ENRICO MARIA SECCI

Perverse Narcissists
and the Impossible Relationships

Surviving love addictions and rediscovering ourselves

youcanprint.it

Original version Title: "I narcisisti perversi e le unioni impossibili -
Sopravvivere alla dipendenza affettiva e ritrovare se stessi"

ISBN | 978-88-92620-34-6

© 2014 by Enrico Maria Secci

English version by Mariano Casti

Cover picture: "Wolves" (2013), from Paola Serino's
photographic project, www.paolaserino.com

© 2016 by Enrico Maria Secci
www.enricomariasecci.blog.tiscali.it

Youcanprint Self-Publishing
Via Roma, 73 - 73039 Tricase (LE) - Italy
www.youcanprint.it
info@youcanprint.it
Facebook: facebook.com/youcanprint.it
Twitter: twitter.com/youcanprintit

Index

The stories told in this book describe clinical cases taken from the Author's professional experience.

To protect the patients' privacy, any personal data which make them recognizable have been omitted.

Each of these stories is reported respecting the privacy of all the people who shared them on my blog, Blog Therapy, at the website address *www.enricomariasecci.blog.tiscali.it.*

The aphorisms which introduce some of the chapters, if not otherwise specified, have been written by the author.

Introduction

Dealing with pathological narcissism and love addictions was not a choice of mine. If I could have chosen, as a human being, I would have preferred not to venture into the abyss of love pains and narcissistic manipulations. But, since the beginning of my career as a psychotherapist, I've started to realize that a lot of patients who came to my office for depressions, anxiety, panic attacks and phobias or other disorders, expressed – through their clinical symptoms – some love issues due to their relationship with a narcissistic partner.

The brief focal psychotherapy effectively reduced the impact of the disorders which led to the request for help and, in about ten sessions, the psychopathological symptoms could completely disappear. I noticed, though, that some of the patients, whose symptoms were disappeared, kept showing up at my office; they were no longer suffering, but were surrounded by a heavy aura, a grey veil, filled with bitterness, dissatisfaction and rage they started to talk about during the therapy sessions.

"Symptoms have disappeared", I told to myself, *"... so, why do they want to go on with the therapy?"* The serious depression was gone, the panic and the terrorizing idea of a sudden death which caused lack of sleep and peace of mind was only a memory... but, even

if they were no longer suffering from the issues which pushed them to my office, the patients kept asking me to go on with the sessions.

A "grey veil" inside the mind

For a long time I have been wondering why once symptoms had disappeared, a persistent air of concern still remained; this justified the need to go on with the therapy.

In the past I thought my job as a clinician was to alienate the symptoms and eliminate the manifest pathology as soon as possible. This still remains my prevailing approach: using all possible means to accelerate and stabilize the change. Neither one session more than necessary, nor one less than needed; but, from the people I've worked with, I have learned that when dealing with a love addiction and/or a pathological narcissist, the psychotherapy cannot be interrupted once the clinical disorders are solved. I have found out that the path can evolve and be completed by processing past emotional experiences and the present, trying to understand and change the pathogenic relationship which, behind the curtains, pulls the strings of the frightening puppet of a "sick" love.

The frequency men and women – once they overcome the pathological emergency – start to talk about their impossible, poisoned and persistent, destructive and desperate relationships with authoritarian and egocentric partners pushed me to study in depth the subject of pathological narcissism and its counterpart: the love addiction.

Still today, I keep observing how the symptom – depression, panic attack, phobia and so on – carries out the double function of both "emotional leash", useful to keep the relationship "impossible", and "message in a bottle", like an SOS sent by the victim after a shipwreck.

The fact that the narcissistic partner reacts with violence after a significant reduction of the symptom – or a total disappearance thanks to the patient's efforts during the therapy – proves the point. The level of well-being reached during the therapy is rejected with sarcasm, derision and contempt, obstructed by starting a couple conflict or compromised by a relational crisis which can be more serious than the past ones.

After a career of more than ten years, my clinical experiences have taught me that narcissists (men or women) respond with a cruel restlessness to the emotional emancipation of their victim. They have a punitive attitude: they opt for provocative and distressing distances, mockery and infidelity so to "mark" the territory, threatened by the disappearance of an issue which gave them a high level of control over their partner. Among the numerous cases which inspired this work, the most relevant and frequent aspect in my patients' stories is the function of the victim's psychic suffering which strengthens - through self-alienation - the "power" the great narcissist needs.

I mean to say that the symptom showed by the "weak" part of the couple represents the emblem of the hegemony of the narcissist part; so, the partner's pain is pursued, wanted or even unconsciously induced, aiming at feeding a magnificent and almighty self-representation at the expense of the partner's stability.

III

The Narcissus' paradox in love relationships

According to this assumption, it can be noticed how a relationship with a perverse narcissist is based on a paradox: *it is possible when impossible*. In order for the relationship to exist, the same has to be constantly destroyed or broken through separation, infidelity and the partner's destruction.

In this book I study this pathogenic paradox and its consequences in a strategic, systemic and relational perspective. Starting from the psychological and psychopathological portrait of the "perverse narcissist" and the love addiction analysis, I focus on the mechanisms which cause, feed and maintain the dysfunctional relationship.

From the blog to the book

"Perverse narcissists and the impossible relationships" is not a psychology essay, neither an academic work nor even a self-help text. This book comes from my experience as a psychotherapist on the Internet and, both in form and content, it can be considered as one of the first Italian blog book on psychology and psychotherapy. Here's the story.

The website Blog Therapy, hosted by the Tiscali platform, was born in 2007 aiming at sharing information on psychology and psychotherapy on the Internet.

Its purpose was to go beyond the stereotype – which is still common – of psychology professionals, who are too often considered as detached oracular consultants or dreams interpreters or even too expensive "paid friends".

During my first year as a blogger, I have written about depression, anxiety and panic attacks, self-esteem disorders and food addictions before publishing the first post on pathological narcissism entitled *Il narcisista perverso*. The following visits and comments explosion, pushed me to study in depth this subject, encouraged by the increasing number of users.

In 2012, the time was right to gather all the posts on love addiction in a book. So, I published *"Gli uomini amano poco - Amore, coppia, dipendenza"*, on love addictions and relational psychology. It was a success, with four reprints in fourteen months and a deluge of messages.

During the last years, pushed by the numerous stories, questions and requests for help made by the Blog Therapy readers, I have been focusing on a particular love addiction case, the specific type in which a narcissistic person has a relationship with a partner, which is the subject of this book.

Part of the contents of *"Perverse narcissists and the impossible relationships"* is composed by posts published on the Internet from 2012 to 2014, reviewed, expanded and completed with unpublished chapters.

In the final section of the book, I explain my clinical and psychotherapeutic approach towards love addictions.
My work method has a strategic and integrated basis; it is a multi-model psychotherapy which involves – in the same perspective – strategic therapy, cognitive behavioral therapy, psychodynamic psychotherapy, narrative therapy, psychoanalysis and Schema Therapy.

In *"Perverse narcissists and the impossible relationships"* I don't mean to have the last word on love pains or narcissistic personality disorder. I don't want to report an endless number of quotations and bibliographical references or put my efforts in some intrapsychic close examinations; I also don't want to venture into metapsychology. Other authors have already been working towards this direction with great effectiveness and expertise.

I hope, though, that the simple format of this blog book can be noticed by the people it has been written for, Blog Therapy and Facebook users included who, while I'm writing, are reaching peaks of 45,000 daily visits.

I also hope to encourage other psychologists and psychotherapists to deal with the subjects of pathological narcissism and love addiction with creativity and dedication.

Enrico Maria Secci

Perverse narcissists
and the impossible relationships

For each ecstatic instant
we must an anguish pay
in keen and quivering ratio,
to the ecstasy.
For each beloved hour
sharp pittances of years,
bitter contested farthings,
and coffers heaped with tears.
(Emily Dickinson)

Phone calls with no answer. No incoming calls or, at least, not when expected. Text messages which seem to get lost within the twists and turns of a Machiavellian unpredictability; then, after hours or days, insignificant and telegraphic replies arrive. A display of insensitivity, indifference and disappointment in response to any request of committing himself in the relationship. He is capable of passionate "impulse" which lasts the exact time to "make love", more or less. Then, again, cryptic, occasional and confused communications are blended with always more arid silences; and if you are so brave to go on, if instead of an urgent and definitive interruption you continue with the relationship, all that comes is: aggressiveness, a constant feeling of uncertainty and danger, pathological jealousy, the desperation caused by the pursuit and derision. These are the typical phenomena of a relationship with a perverse narcissist, a man who - often beyond his awareness - acts in a destructive way and pushes the partner towards the love addiction.

Control and lack of commitment

In relational addictions, the concept of "perverse narcissist" does not describe a personality pathology, but a way of building sentimental relationships based on control over the partner and lack of commitment. This means that the perverse narcissist cannot be always considered as a pathological subject; he can rather be a person who opts for strategies coherent with his basic purpose: to feed his self-esteem at the partner's expense and with a minimum effort. Towards the "victims" – who look for an intense and long-lasting love relationship – the narcissist feels indifferent. Whenever the narcissist faces a confrontation, he can look as annoyed or act violently.

From his own perspective – which lacks of empathy -, the perverse narcissist cannot fully understand the partner's needs and sees her requests as disproportionate and unjustified. By trying to understand and listen, he would lose control and supremacy over the partner. For this reason, those who insist on continuing the relationship with a perverse narcissist do not have any hope of success and unwittingly act in a self-destructive way.

There are no acts, persuasions, sacrifices, changes or strategies which can turn the perverse narcissist into a Prince charming;

however, the obsession which affects and subjugates the victims - sometimes for years, sometimes for the entire life – consists in the possibility of being replaced by more beautiful women who maybe can be more capable of making themselves loved. The belief of being responsible for the pathological partner's oppressive behavior and the tendency to self-blame for the relationship unhappiness are the victims' constant characteristics.

Objectification and interchangeability

The perverse narcissist's "psychological game" is based on the objectification or reification principle, which means converting people into "objects". He knows the partner's weight, height, size, colors, phrases and attitudes, and gets angry whenever the characteristics do not match with his ideal model, taken as indisputable parameter.

So, the perverse narcissist can never get enough: the partner's appearance is always inadequate: her dresses, voice tone, subjects, friendships, ideas, schedules are wrong… the partner's present and past.

At the beginning of the relationship, the perverse narcissist usually hides his restlessness and intolerance. But, as the relationship goes on, he conquers always a wider margin of manoeuvre and pushes the partner towards always bigger conflicts and humiliations, as if he wanted to measure his own power.

The victim's desperate reactions are rewarding and reassuring.

Sometimes he can be moved by the prostration showed by the partner and tries to "remedy" with some cuddles and promises to change. These repairing behaviors make the victim more confused and feed her addiction, since they make the love illusion grow.

So, who is the perverse narcissist? First of all, it is useful to say that he is neither a magnetic Dorian Grey not a dark and handsome man nor a beautiful and damned as suggested by film stereotypes. On the contrary, he is often shallow, mediocre, soaked with stereotypes and obsessed by the need for other people to like him; a person oppressed by the idea that someone could unmask him. He is like an erasable blackboard: you can write whatever you want on it, but nothing remains permanently. One day he's an attentive and kind lover, the day after he's a fugitive; sometimes he's a poet, sometimes a lout. Too busy in his psychological tightrope walking to realize that he's causing a disaster; but he's pleased with the sentimental pursuit he causes.

Idealization and egocentrism

Those who get caught in a love addiction with a perverse narcissist, are initially seduced by the confidence the partner seems to choose them with. Right afterwards, though, ambivalence and inconstancy appear within the relationship: the despairing alternation of silences and aggressiveness which is typical of this kind of love addictions.

The ambiguity of the narcissistic communication is so significant that it can be interpreted in an egocentric way by the victim, according to his or her values and expectations.

The hardest challenge for those who fall into the love addiction vortex with a perverse narcissist is learning how to translate - according to a different reality model - messages which seem to encourage the relationship but actually aim at freezing it in a comfortable and free "balance" which gratifies the narcissist's great image. In this case, the victim is guilty of putting herself aside and surrender to the partner's will, manipulations and lies; the victims is unconsciously guilty of dancing the dark and chaotic tango of condescension, confusion and illusion. To keep the partner within the borders of her idea of love, the victim builds castles in the sky which are destined to collapse: she idealizes the lover to the point of creating the myth of the perfect man who, hence, she does not deserve. So, she blames herself. "I'm a loser", "Everybody is better than me", "He hesitates because he knows that I'm not good. He will find someone better than me and will fall in love with her".

The negative thoughts - which seem to be "logical" if compared to the emotional experiences they derive from – represent, an illusory attempt to "save the partner's idea" and attribute the relationship failure to mistakes she has presumably made.

In this case, the victim has the illusion of control: she has the idea that changing her own behaviors will be enough to win her loved one over.

Behaviors to avoid

Generally, there are three types of behavior which maintain the addiction and lead the relationship towards a potentially infinite series of pursuits and traumas:

1. attempting to unmask the perverse narcissist;

5

2. asking for explanations;
3. keeping the communication open.

The love addiction is the consequence of recurring dysfunctional communication patterns which grow stronger in a context of distorted expectations on the same love relationship. So, we are not dealing with an individual problem related to the past of the subjects – especially their childhood –, but with a pathology which exists in the present, in the "here and now" of the relationship: unconsciously, in the present, love addicted people are prisoners of thoughts, emotions and behaviors deriving from a mutual actions-responses system, not necessarily from big traumas deriving from past experiences of one of the partners.

Those who start psychotherapy to search for the remote causes of the vicious circle they are trapped in, run the risk of forgetting about current problems and complicating their condition. Love addicted people's tendency is to blame themselves for not being loved and constantly search for "something broken within themselves", in spite of recognizing the partner's faults within the relationship. When the partner acts as a perverse narcissist, the victim's inadequacy sense reaches very high peaks; the narcissist moves within the relationship only to feed his great self and doesn't hesitate to destroy the fragile image of the counterpart. Recognizing and identifying the perverse narcissist's behaviors are functional to gradually define the idealized image the victim has in mind and - in a short period of time - to change the communication which feeds the love addiction.

The three mistakes which feed the addiction

First of all, what discourages the victim is the difficulty in clearly identifying the uselessness of her own actions within the relationship and surrendering to the idea that whatever she does is wrong. There is no way to make the partner fall in love. Even when the narcissist seems to get closer, he suddenly turns back; even when he seems to give love, he is manipulating. That's it! He manipulates because he doesn't tolerate to lose control, being abandoned and, above all, being unmasked in his emotional inability. This is the first mistake to avoid: trying to unmask the partner by clearly talking about his egoism, inconstancy, the cruelty of his silences and the violence of his disappearances. To protect his own positive image, the narcissist will defend himself by convincing the partner of being inadequate and crazy, and justifying his behaviors as reactions to her inadequacy; he can also temporarily fulfill the victim's needs just to show her that she is wrong; then, he will suddenly come back to his usual sadistic and non-affective behavior. In this situation, any attempt to unmask the narcissist leads to the recurring relationship pattern and feeds the obsession.

To really get out of this condition, it is necessary to forget about the need to hear apologies and admissions from the partner and act in an autonomous way. This will only be the first step, since when the perverse narcissist feels that the prey is losing interest, he puts all his efforts into catching her again. The narcissist is capable of showing up after months or years to take the control again. In order to do it, he can ask for explanations, act as a friend or in a seductive way. The second mistake to avoid is accepting to "give explanations" about the situation face-to-face, knowing that it is a trap. It is a tough decision for the victim because, more or less consciously, she can succumb to the charm of a person who was supposed to despise her, and who suddenly has an open attitude on the relationship. The key word is "No". No dates, no "explanations", it is better to have nothing to do with the other person anymore, at least until the path of liberation and emancipation from the addiction is completed.

The third mistake to avoid is to keep the communication with the perverse narcissist open. No texting, no Facebook, no direct or indirect contacts are the key to overcome the emotional abstinence and close the relationship once and for all. In fact, it is not possible to "recover together" from a love addiction when caused by narcissism; it cannot absolutely be a joint path, but the result of an individual "process" experienced by the "victim" who, recognizing the partner's patterns, comes to the conclusion that the same relationship was actually impossible.

Recognizing the narcissism

Historically, the concept of narcissism in psychoanalysis was born from the need to understand sexual perversions (sadism, masochism, exhibitionism, voyeurism etc.) which nowadays we call paraphilias. Narcissism has evolved outside the sexual sphere to become one of the most important and controversial subjects in psychotherapy.

The first studies on narcissistic disorders date back to 1892, when Havelock Ellis, for the first time, used the Greek myth as a key to understand autoerotism. But it was Freud who "officially baptized" narcissism with *An Introduction to Narcissism*, 1914; this was the reference point for successive studies, clinical observations and hundreds of publications which, for the first time in 1980, have led to the narcissistic personality disorder codification in the third edition of the Diagnostic and Statistical Manual of Mental Disorders (DSM-III).

The inclusion of narcissism in the DSM highlights eight diagnostic criteria, among which at least five have to be identified to formulate a narcissistic personality disorder diagnosis:

- reaction to criticism through anger, shame or humiliation;
- tendency to take advantage of other people for their own personal interest;

- sense of grandiosity, which means the sensation of feeling important, even if not deserved;
- the subjects feel unique or special, as if only a few people could understand them;
- limitless success, power, love, beauty fantasies etc.;
- the subjects feel as they deserve privileges more than the other people;
- excessive attention or admiration requests;
- lack of empathy towards other people's problems.

In the 1987 revision of the Manual (DSM-II-R) another criterion was added to make the diagnosis more accurate according to observations and clinical researches:

- persistent envy.

Speaking of "narcissism" as a single disorder is an oversimplification, since after the conceptualization made by the American Psychiatric Association, the term has been used to define a personality disorder or a personality characteristic; terms such as "narcissistic wounds", "narcissistic trauma" or "narcissistic defenses" refer to unconscious dynamics not necessarily related to a psycho-affective disorder.

As we will see in the following pages, the clinicians and researchers' intention is to find an integrated and dynamic perspective on narcissisms; this permits to share diagnostic criteria and create effective and efficient therapeutic models both at an individual level and within the relationship between the narcissist and "victim".

Freud, Kohut, Kernberg and Lowen: four perspectives on narcissism

From the centuries-old debate on narcissism we have come to define a complex psychological structure at the border between physiology and pathology.

Freud describes a primary narcissism as the phase of psycho-sexual development which precedes the construction of the Self. During the early childhood, the individual is temporarily unable to distinguish himself from the outside world and his attachment figures; he lives in such a state of perceptive fusion that he sees other people and the surrounding environments as extensions of himself.

During this archaic, egocentric and "Ptolemaic" phase, the child sees himself as a love object; then he discovers the world is not inside himself after the first loneliness and frustration experiences. Then, the child becomes aware of the impossibility of being self-sufficient as part of a huge human planet.

So, narcissism can be considered as a temporary and physiological phase of the psychic development which can turn into pathology (secondary narcissism) after traumatic events faced during the childhood, especially when the mother's emotional function is insufficient.

Kohut (1977) highlighted the importance of primary relationships between child and parents – especially with mothers – in determining the transition to a non-pathological function; this implies the abandonment of narcissistic strategies in favor of an integrated and empathic personality towards ourselves, the other people and the outside world.

From the Kohut perspective, a functional narcissism exists: a personality nucleus which is the origin of the individual's ambition and creativity. So, this narcissism has to be considered as healthy. The pathological narcissistic Self construction during the adulthood would represent, though, the defensive and maladaptive reaction to one or more emotional disappointments - experienced as a child - caused by the attachment figures or other significant people, adults or peers such as classmates and friends. The narcissist portrait painted by Khout describes a vulnerable, incomplete and suffering individual.

Kernberg's theory (1975, 1987) described three types of narcissism: an infantile narcissism, a healthy narcissism and a pathological narcissism. The narcissistic pathology appears when a person is unable to integrate the idealized image of his Self into the outside world and other people's vision; so, he hides himself in grandiosity fantasies which diminish the ability to adapt to the complexity of emotional relationships.

Lowen (1983) as well considers the narcissistic disorder as the result of a lack of integration of negative and traumatic feelings deriving from the first experiences into the Self; he focuses on the way the first emotional deprivations affect both the individual's psychological functioning and the physical experiences. Lowen expands the narcissism study and comprehension from the intra-psychic and relational sphere to the physical dimension, by using the following activities during the therapy: observation and analysis of breathing, posture, muscular tension and rigidity which are signals of the emotional conflict the narcissist is trapped in.

This quick overview cannot include all the international publications on narcissism. The debate on narcissistic personality is so complex that the scientific community have considered the possibility to remove the Narcissistic Personality Disorder from the fifth and very recent edition of the Diagnostic and Statistical Manual of Mental Disorders (2014).

If it wasn't for the heated protest of clinicians and researchers from all parts of the world during the drafting phase of the "Psychiatrist Bible", the narcissistic personality disorder removal would have been considered as a sort of an unjustified scientific "pardon".

The removal of a so important category such as the pathological narcissism from the DSM-V would have complicated both the diagnosis and the psychotherapeutic treatment; above all, it would have compromised the crucial debate among specialists on a disorder which most of the psychotherapists encounter on a daily basis, both directly in narcissistic patients and indirectly, by observing the consequences of their actions on people who fall in the trap of a narcissist and ask for help.

The Narcissistic Personality Disorder in the DSM-V

At page 775 of the Diagnostic and Statistical Manual of Mental Disorders, Italian edition, which has been recently published by Raffaello Cortina Editore, there are the diagnostic criteria of pathological narcissism, which are not so different from those reported in the previous editions:

- Has a grandiose sense of self-importance (e.g., exaggerates achievements and talents, expects to be recognized as superior without commensurate achievements).
- Is preoccupied with fantasies of unlimited success, power, brilliance, beauty, or ideal love.
- Believes that he or she is "special" and unique and can only be understood by, or should associate with, other special or high-status people (or institutions).
- Requires excessive admiration.
- Has a sense of entitlement (i.e., unreasonable expectations of especially favorable treatment or automatic compliance with his or her expectations).
- Is interpersonally exploitative (i.e., takes advantage of others to achieve his or her own ends).
- Lacks empathy: is unwilling to recognize or identify with the feelings and needs of others.
- Is often envious of others or believes that others are envious of him or her.
- Shows arrogant, haughty behaviors or attitudes.

From a general point of view, the diagnostic indicators form a pattern of grandiosity which constitutes the key of the pathological narcissist's profile.

The Manual estimates, for this disorder, a prevalence of 6.2% in samples considered as representative of the population; relatively to those who have been diagnosed with narcissistic personality disorder, 50%-75% are male

The DSM highlights the contradictions experienced by the narcissist: grandiosity acts as a counterbalance of the extreme vulnerability, the inadequacy feelings, social and emotional incapability of a person who often lives suspended between moments of self-exaltation and a deep loneliness.

A further diagnostic indicator is the substances abuse: tobacco, alcohol and cocaine and so on, can constitute an attempt of self-therapy aiming at relieving the constant anxiety and dissatisfaction typical in this pathology (Narcissistic Personality Disorder).

The narcissist's profile is described in three pages and fulfills the requirement adopted in the manual, a reference for most part of the psychiatric and psychotherapy professionals. It is clearly a pragmatic criterion which is also restrictive: it is very far from reality, where the clinician encounters shades and varieties of narcissism which can partially include diagnostic criteria and are also related to a wide narcissistic spectrum, which is more complex than the one defined by the Manual.

Recently, Kernberg casted doubts on the validity of the categorial approach used by the DSM in favor of a dimensional vision, a more realistic perspective aiming to a change rather than a diagnosis.

Narcissistic psychology is divided in so many levels that it results elusive for psychiatric nosography, which needs "stable" rather than ambiguous references to formulate diagnosis. Furthermore, the pathological narcissism - which does not cause pain to those who suffer from it, but it does to people who are in contact with the narcissist - can hardly be considered as a psychopathology.

Three types of narcissism: Behary's contribution

One of the most interesting contemporary authors, Wendy T. Behary (2012) describes three types of narcissism: healthy narcissism, covert maladaptive narcissism and overt maladaptive narcissism:

- **Healthy narcissism** describes a socially integrated individual, capable of balancing egocentrism with empathy, generosity and altruism. The healthy narcissist is not only inoffensive in emotional relationships, but he is also considered as a resource or a leader by other people.
- **Covert narcissism.** Covert narcissist appears as a virtuous person, a champion of justice, a hero who defends morality and keeps to the straight and narrow in a world of ignorant and ungrateful people. He puts all of his efforts into appearing better than the others and denigrates them for their weaknesses and mistakes.
- **Overt narcissism.** The overt narcissist lives in a self-exaltation state, in the constant attempt to be accepted by the others. He only cares about people who support him and destroys or ignores anyone who could ruin his grandiosity halo (very often imaginary).

The narcissistic continuum

The types described by Behary seem to belong to a *continuum*, a "narcissistic spectrum" which goes from the "healthy and functional" polarity to the "maladaptive" one. Within this *continuum*, there are infinite shades of narcissism. So, the need to "think in the plural" is better explained in a multi-dimensional way so to get out of the chaos of love addictions.

Therefore, not all narcissists are dangerous. On the contrary, "healthy" narcissists can be excellent poets, artists, managers, socially active doctors or extraordinary leaders without harming anyone.

It is useful to learn how to recognize the violent faces of covert or overt maladaptive narcissism and work on them to stop their dramatic influence on love relationships and, above all, to face their most radical consequence: the love addiction.

How to unmask the perverse narcissist

To unmask the perverse narcissist, first of all, two variables have to be taken into account: self-esteem and sociability.

In the most dangerous perverse narcissist, these two dimensions are inversely proportional: the self-esteem is expressed through self-exaltation and self-ostentation, need of absolute control, cruel and caustic criticism. On the other hand, sociability – exhibited whether possible - is scarce, shallow and false.

The perverse narcissist does not sincerely care about friends, unless they are useful for his purposes; he considers people he cannot act as a grand predator with as totally invisible. For instance, heterosexual male perverse narcissists completely deny the others' identity; they behave as if the others did not exist and they hardly maintain disinterested friendships. The same thing can be confirmed for female perverse narcissists: they feel as the other women were envious of them; they usually feel rancor and aggressiveness towards other women, while men usually ignore their possible rivals.

The higher is the self-exaltation level, the lower is the sociability; as a result, narcissism moves towards the maladaptive area of the narcissistic *continuum*.

Even if the perverse narcissist seems to be unaware of his social inadequacy and loneliness, at some level he feels the distress caused by isolation; he is ashamed of it and often lies to hide it.

A first suggestion to unmask him is learning how to ask questions about his relationships, friends, family, in a sensitive, respectful and empathic way, trying not to use an interrogative tone. The more perverse the narcissist is, the more he is likely to be elusive, rude, violent and punitive. The more perverse he is, the more he is likely to wiggle out of the communication by suddenly interrupting it; he can turn the interlocutor into the subject of the discussion, blaming her for his or her "inappropriate and gross" curiosity.

Am I dealing with a pathological narcissist?

Please, read the following statements and attribute each a score, from 0 to 2:

0 = never
1= rarely
2 = always

Keep in mind that there are no "correct" or "incorrect" answers. Please, answer exclusively according to your experience and be as honest as possible.

Questionnaire

1. He acts as he was the center of the universe.

   [0] [1] [2]

2. He expects to be treated with special regard.

   [0] [1] [2]

3. He makes uncompromising decisions.

[0] [1] [2]

4. He tends to deny the obvious.

[0] [1] [2]

5. I have never heard him saying "I'm sorry", "I apologize".

[0] [1] [2]

6. In front of other people, he does not hesitate to ridicule me or to treat me with sarcasm.

[0] [1] [2]

7. Basically, he does not have real friends.

[0] [1] [2]

8. If he desires something, he stubbornly expects to get it.

[0] [1] [2]

9. He is jealous without any reason.

[0] [1] [2]

10. He wants to know about all my movements but does not want to tell me about his.

[0] [1] [2]

11. He is very demanding towards the others.

[0] [1] [2]

12. He is very hard on himself.

[0] [1] [2]

13. He punishes me with silence.

[0] [1] [2]

14. He easily gets offended and reacts through personal attacks.

[0] [1] [2]

15. He thinks to be better than the others.

[0] [1] [2]

16. Very often, he finds other people boring.

[0] [1] [2]

17. He excessively dwells on details or has "fixations"

[0] [1] [2]

18. He smokes or drinks a lot, or takes drugs.

[0] [1] [2]

19. He is obsessed with physical appearance.

[0] [1] [2]

20. He is almost cruel when judging other people's physical appearance.

[0] [1] [2]

21. He seems to be emotionless.

[0] [1] [2]

22. When watching a touching movie or during moving situations he becomes insensitive.

[0] [1] [2]

23. He feels no remorse after mistreating me.

[0] [1] [2]

24. He constantly asks for others people's acceptance.

[0] [1] [2]

25. He naturally lies to look superior.

[0] [1] [2]

26. He becomes angry and violent when I'm sad.

[0] [1] [2]

27. When he notices I'm happy, he gets sad or attacks me.

[0] [1] [2]

28. Every time he receives a "no" as an answer, he gets literally furious.

[0] [1] [2]

29. Although he tries not to show it, he frequently looks depressed.

[0] [1] [2]

30. He is vindictive and doesn't know forgiveness.

[0] [1] [2]

From 0 to 25 points

According to your perception, your partner is well-balanced and he or she cares about your needs. Perhaps, sometimes you feel as if he or she is "inattentive" and a bit more of jealousy would be good for your relationship. If your score is too close to zero, the risk for your relationship is to going on under an excessive control, and eventually, this can diminish the capability to share your emotional needs and fulfill them by cooperating.

From 26 to 45 points

Your partner displays some narcissistic characteristic; so, paying more attention to your relationship quality could be useful. Do you have a mutual and balanced relationship? Do you often fight? How do you evaluate your relationship so far?

The higher the score is, the higher is the probability for you to feel entrapped; so you could realize, at least partially, that this relationship makes you frustrated and if it wasn't for your patience it would be over.

From 45 to 60 points

Red Alert. Stop and ask yourself what you are doing. Maybe, your relationship is unbalanced and the lack of reciprocity causes constant fights and a certain submissive suffering from you. Think about a possible lack of clear and shared private spaces and the fact that the relationship is not going well, despite all your efforts. Do you feel safe with him/her? Has he or she been showing you to be honest and reliable so far? Are you happy?

What are your relations with the outside world? What do you have in common?

The human monster

*The most loved tyrant
is the one who rewards and punishes you without a reason.*
(Ennio Flaiano)

Love addiction cases are always shocking, since they push their protagonists into a self-destruction vortex it seems they are not willing to get out from, despite the pain escalation it causes. Logic reasoning would make think that infidelity, lies, psychological abuse - sometimes veiled, sometimes clear - and verbal or physical violence which characterize the addiction push the victim to interrupt the relationship, but, from a psycho-logical perspective, often the opposite occurs.

Indeed, each fault and attack from the "strong" part of the couple causes the apparently unexplainable effect to strengthen the relationship, while it erodes the responsive capability of the victim who surrenders to an exasperating love.

The ambivalence trap

People trapped in love addictions live subjugated by ambivalence: the partner sometimes is kind, romantic, charming, unique and special... sometimes becomes cruel, cold, unapproachable, mean, trivial. The object of the addiction shows two seamless but contrasting faces, blended in a poisonous alchemy; this last sentence says a lot about the impossibility to understand if he or she is totally good or bad, which is quite paralyzing.

We think both men and women who are incapable of giving love are cold, calculating and non-affective people, emotional criminals who act in a suspicious and unequivocal way; but this is not the case at all. On the contrary, in love addictions, at least one of the partners shows a double identity and alternates emotional rushes – with a child's disarming spontaneity – with bursts of rage or icy silences; he or she makes vibrant promises of love, then denies with inconceivable vehemence.

This duality constitutes the fulcrum of the relational addiction: the "victim" falls in love with the partner's positive face, with his or her sentimental part and temporary sensitivity; the partner idealizes the narcissist and totally dedicates himself/herself to him/her, minimizing or denying the "negative" part; this last part is separate from the love object, since it is illogical and inconsistent with his/her conscious emotional needs and the idea of a romantic love. The monster which chains, mistreat, humiliates, manipulates, takes advantage of his/her is safe, under the protection of his prisoner who blames himself/herself for any punishment or violence suffered. The victim also forgives the partner for everything and lets everything go by, so to catch a glimpse of a fleeting angelic light on his/her loved one's face.

Monsters don't exist, or at least, they don't exist in the stereotypical shape we all have in our mind. Human monsters, the real ones, don't have a vampire's sharp teeth, nor frightening physical deformities; they don't emanate putrid smelling and are not armed to the teeth. They have grounded certainties and tell the solemn truth. Their secret consists in separating and isolating "negative" emotions from themselves as much as possible: fear of being abandoned, vulnerability, the potential fallacy of emotions, choices and actions, fear of succumbing to the anguish of being human.

So, if the love addicted sees the partner as an angel fallen into an hypnotic nebula of opposite and moving feelings, the monster perceives himself/herself as a perfect human being undeservedly offended by the partner's fragility and his/her obscene devotion.

The more the partner exposes himself/herself to and fights the pain caused by an impossible love, the more the monster feels rage and contempt.

The fundamental mistake

Basically, the drama of love addiction starts from a huge misunderstanding. The "victim" falls in love with an angelic and charming face; he/she thinks the human monster's appearances are caused by his/her being unworthy. He/she is subjected to accusations, victim of sinister lies and clear infidelity, with the illusion of being loved by the partner's positive face; he/she desires the partner to get out of the dark evil which infects him/her. But the intemperance and the anxiety which come out from the loved one's marvelous mask, the savage contempt, the mean indolence and his/her icy behaviors are not the mask of a good and sweet person: these are the faces of a human monster.

The real monster is dual, lives inside a contradiction, embodies it; he/she is the result of a failed integration between positive and negative parts of himself/herself, of his/her emotional past, the deleted, traumatic and never-analyzed experiences as a tormented child.

The love disease

All mistakes in love have to be paid for.
It is good to know it.

A lot of people ask me: "How can I make the perverse narcissist fall in love with me, how can I make him fall in love with me again?". Other people, sadly ask me: "How can I take my revenge for all he did to me?". These are crucial and frequent matters when facing and recovering from a love addiction, since "I want to make him pay" or "I want to win him over again" are actually opposite parts of the same feeling which still conserves its pathogenic potential. When a love relationship gets sick and makes us sick, it turns into obsession; obsession is the distinguishing feature of the love addiction, independently of the different ways it appears.

Recognizing the obsession is easy: our thoughts are full of it, our mind gets stuck in recurring contents, our emotions gathers around a nucleus (winning him over again, jealousy, sense of guilt, revenge) and form dangerous vortexes like water running down the pipes; our behavior becomes repetitive, all things become meaningless.

The love disease is the love addiction, the inability to free ourselves from unsatisfying, painful, often oppressive and humiliating relationships; from an empty and cold relationship which story is often interrupted by long silences, laconic and insignificant text messages, disappointed expectations and lack of communication. Brooding over the past seems to be a step forward, but it is a sign of a covert addiction, similar to the clear symptom of obsession.

Revenge or a new attempt of love conquest?

In spite of their clear diversity, revenge and conquest have in common a significant base which constitutes the addiction core: the illusion that actions can eventually influence the partner's feelings and the tendency to use them to arouse an emotional effect. The love addicted cannot accept the fact that the pathological relationship – wrongly called "love" – is based on an almost complete lack of reciprocity and the evident distortion of the expectations on the love object. Lack of reciprocity means that the individuals trapped in the "love disease" think, feel and act only taking into account their own point of view and unconsciously interact not with the other people, but with an ideal image of them. For this reason, the love addiction stories are characterized by shocking events: little misunderstandings turn into incurable wounds, love displays are ignored, the cruelest infidelities and the meanest words are quickly "forgotten" and covered by the promise to start over again. So, the nexus "healthy and functional" - which connects people through appropriate actions and reactions – is no longer valid.

For example, in a love relationship, the partner's ambiguity and uncertainties can cause pain to the other person; but, after a certain period of time, it leads to the self-defensive reaction to interrupt the relationship, decision which denotes respect for himself/herself and the partner's feelings. In a love addiction, though, emotional ambiguity and uncertainties showed by one part of the couple cause a bigger attachment, tiring love chases and stubborn attempts to persuade the partner through seduction strategies, psychological tricks, veiled or clear blackmails and other "irrational" behaviors which violate both partners' integrity. In any case, there is a fail in describing realistically the partner; there is a fail in rejecting him/her when he/she — as a different individual — acts in a dangerous way for the partner's mental stability.

The illusory solution.

People trapped in the maze of the love disease experience the tragedy of trying to think with the other's head, not realizing that they're thinking with their own one. When a relationship is source of a so intense pain and tragic consequences such those of love addictions, the possibility not to understand the partner has to be accepted. It also takes to give up looking for "logical reasons", since these would follow their own logic, which is not the partner's one. Using our own head, identifying and fulfilling our emotional needs, looking for satisfying and possible relationships: these simple things, in a love addiction are huge obstacles. So, since changing the partner is impossible, we come to the illusory solution: to work on ourselves, by repressing our feelings, controlling ourselves, not listening to what we need, punishing ourselves with the firm belief that this is the right way that leads to a sort of a love relationship. It seems absurd, but in the psychology of emotional addictions, this choice is ruled by the same logic which maintains and feeds the pathology: the complete absence of self-consideration, the belief not to be a valuable person and the symbiotic idealization with the partner, considered as a sort of magical and powerful totem the victim has to kneel down before, hoping for the miracle of Love.

"Winning without fighting" is an ancient strategy of the art of war and it can be adopted when, as occurs in love addictions, the war becomes the essence of the relationship. Leaving the battlefield, interrupting any strategy and communication with the enemy is the way to defeat it. It is, therefore, useless trying to take a revenge or find strategies for the "re-conquest". The real victory is learning to "let go" what does not work, what hurts and causes pain, to take care and protect ourselves from psychological traps, illusions and future and present assailants.

Inside the perverse narcissist's mind

*Narcissism does not consists,
as commonly believed,
of an incapability to love,
but in the incapability to accept
the other's love.*

Psychopathologies are frequently caused by the lack of sense, the impossibility to find a sort of coherence, an acceptable meaning in what we are experiencing. As human beings, within the relational and emotional sphere we feel the urgent need to understand the reason of a specific behavior; so we often decide to opt for linear or causal logics, which presupposes the cause and effect existence. For example: "If I'm caring and attentive (cause) the partner will reward me with love (effect)"; "If the partner refuses me (effect) it means that I've done something wrong or something is wrong with me (cause)". Causal logic provides an oversimplified pattern of relational dynamics which is less effective as the interactive context gets more complex. In fact, human relationships are based on a psycho-logic which is very different from linear logic. Communication is a circular process (Watzlawick et al., 1974) where "causes" and "effects" basically do not exist, but constitute an arbitrary reduction of complexity into linear "if... then" segments, which we use to make our life simpler and easily move within an unknown universe composed by our psychology, the partner's one and the infinite results derived from the interaction between these spheres.

Relational problem-solving features

Each interpersonal conflict, each psychological crisis, each traumatic event within the relationship (like infidelity episodes, a separation etc.) puts the "linear theories" – theories on the reality we have experienced during past relationships - through the wringer and diminishes their general validity. So, we start searching for reasons (causes), thinking that doing this way we could stop and solve the consequences of an emotional disaster. When the problem regards the relationship with the partner, one of the more common mistakes is trying to understand the reasons of his or her actions, assuming that his or her mind works like ours and unconsciously using our way of perceive reality to search for possible solutions. The remedies deriving from this type of strategy, usually, "make the evil worst" since they are based on the implicit belief that the partner thinks the same way we do, shares the same beliefs and values. Interpreting the partner's communications according to our own point of view causes an increase of the distance and makes the conflict worse. Vice versa, when we talk about how we perceive a specific situation and the partner gives us explanations on his or her personal past experiences, it becomes easier to find effective solutions which can be satisfying to both.

It's not about "why" but "how"

Generally, the reasons "why" for both partners partially represent the relationship reality and, once shared, they help to understand that the problem is caused by a series of communicative distortions and mutual misunderstandings. An attempt to discover how both partners have co-created the conflict conditions – in most part of the cases – can lead to a solution and makes the relationship stronger.

These brief mentions on interpersonal problem-solving are valid whether the partners consider themselves as involved in the relationship, whether there is mutual interest and esteem.

In case of a love-addicted relationship, dedication, interest and value equality lack from the beginning: the relationship is based on a strong and strict complementarity, where a partner perceives himself or herself as (or he or she actually is) the "prevailing" one, while the other partner, more or less consciously, recognizes this definition and strives to get love and acceptance. This occurs because the "weak" partner acts in good faith, wrongly presuming that "if I will be patient and I will behave properly (cause), my partner will change (consequence)"; "my partner ignores me, mistreats me or punishes me (consequence) because I'm not or I don't do enough" (consequence).

"Cause distortion" in love addictions

It is clear that the causal logic adopted by the addicted partner to solve a so unbalanced and frustrating relationship causes linear sequences which are all detrimental to her: these sequences exclusively highlight her faults, not taking into account her partner's mistakes and faults. This - when the counterpart displays narcissistic features - further highlights the power the partner perceives and makes the relationship asymmetry grow. Then, if the partner is a narcissist, everything turns into a cruel game, a constant pillory, a perverse court which definitively convicts the victim, forced to suffer for her presumed and consensual inadequacy, always believing that after all this pain, love will come.

A double-blind relationship

The problem is that in love addictions, the relationship doesn't exist and nobody realizes it. I mean, the love addicted ends up totally focusing on himself/herself, on her "faults", pains, losing the realistic perceptions of the "subject" she "loves", who turns into an object, a totem, a utopia; nothing similar to the original narcissist who is instable and detached from reality and relationship.

In the narcissist's mind, the partner doesn't exist as an interlocutor, as a person; he/she is just a mirror, a tool to confirm the image he/she has of himself/herself and makes his/her ego grow; the narcissist's ego needs sacrifices to his tyrannical and sovereign personality.

The narcissist and his/her partner are two blind people, unable to see each other, doomed to believe in the existence of a "love" which is only the terrifying projection of the inability to love someone within a different psychological reality: a satisfying and shared reality.

Issues, traumas and fears

Both the narcissist and the "victim" are psychologically extraneous, alienated, totally isolated from each other; they try to solve a relational problem which doesn't exist because that very relationship doesn't; it can only exist as an unconscious alibi to avoid to definitively face the actual problem: the relationship with themselves, the perception of their own Self, each with a personal history full of discontinuity, fears, traumas and significant choices to be made.

Understanding narcissism through the myth

According to the myth, Narcissus was a young and really handsome man; his beauty was irresistible. He died drowned in a spring, enchanted by the beauty of his own reflection he fell in love with. Mythology recounts a fascinating and complex story which describes a proud and haughty boy, who used to seduce men and women of any age. Besides the Ovid's version, ancient documents report precious details of this myth which allow us to understand its universal evocative power and cultural influence; these details permit to study the personality disorder which owes its name to the tragic character of this story: narcissism.

Narcissus' family.

Narcissus was born from a violent relationship. His father Cesiphus, god of the river with the same name, raped and abducted the spring nymph Leiriope to possess her beauty. This is an interesting feature, since also in reality narcissists are conceived and raised within a painful and quite unbalanced relationship; when he is not used to fulfill the affective needs of one of his parents, he lives in a self-exaltation condition deriving from the great attentions his family gives to him. Often, the narcissist's parents impose peremptory rules and very high standards the child has to respect to receive love from them. "You must be perfect otherwise we won't love you", they seem to constantly repeat. So, narcissism can be considered as a childish attempt not to succumb to the affective confusion, not to break up and disappear into the inadequacy sense deriving from one or both parents' requests.

Returning to the Narcissus' myth, it is likely that his tyrannical, violent and possessive father Cesiphus represents the real perverse narcissist precursor, since he cruelly imprisoned the compliant nymph who, after being raped, gave birth to Narcissus. This is another connection the myth has with psychology and psychiatry notions: it is also frequent in real life that narcissists have or have had a narcissist parent.

The emotional tragedy of his family seems to totally penetrate into Narcissus, until his tragic ending: a death in water, a drowning in a spring which, if analytically observed, makes think to an unconscious attempt to join his mother Leiriope (the spring nymph) or to follow the same destiny by getting swallowed by the waters the same way she let Cesiphus – the river god – imprison her.

From this point of view, Narcissus and narcissists are similar: they miserably drown into an unsolved and impossible love, repeating – unconsciously and in a distorted way – the patterns learned during the childhood, which have never been recognized.

Narcissus during his puberty.

Ovid tells about an adolescent Narcissus who seduces men and women, all atrociously rejected. Like narcissists, Narcissus doesn't know empathy: he shows indifference to all the sentimental and human consequences of his behavior; on the contrary, he seems to be pleased with the pain he causes. At a clinical level as well, the narcissist despise the other people; everybody looks inferior, silly, ungrateful, unworthy and the violence he humiliates them with is equal to the rage for the inability to love someone else. This rage is entirely addressed to the neighbor, to the other people who are guilty of leaving him alone because of their disappointing pettiness. He's doomed to loneliness.

Narcissus is desperately alone with his handsomeness, prisoner of his father's arrogance and haughtiness, and his mother's submission. The same way Cesiphus subjugates Leiriope, Narcissus – in a rough and cruel identification with the river god – destroys whoever gives love to him.

Somehow, Narcissus seems to participate in a cruel competition with his father, a power game which pushes him to do worse than his father did. Another recurring feature in clinical psychology: narcissists are involved – since their childhood – in a love-hate relationship with a father perceived as powerful, almost non-affective, severe and oppressive; or with an absent father, separated by his wife or even deceased and then idealized and perceived as a demigod. They hate their father but, since he controls his mother, they unconsciously learn how to internalize it and compete with him in terms of control and destruction. For this reason, they can become perverse.

The Aminia murder

The Ovid's version of Narcissus' story is the most famous one, but Conon adds a fundamental and terrifying episode to this legend. Conon recounts of Aminia, a boy who fell in love with Narcissus; unlike the others, he did not surrender to the Narcissus' refusal and stubbornly fought to win him over. So, Narcissus gave him his sword and asked him to stab himself as an extreme demonstration of love. Aminia killed himself but, at the moment he was about to die, cursed Narcissus by invoking the Gods. This dramatic episode of the myth shows another recurring feature in the perverse narcissists' life: before oppressing women, they have experienced emotional homoaffective relationships - with ambivalence and indifference –, which led to destroy their partners who, just like Arminia, were pushed to the self-destruction paradox.

Speaking further about the parallelism between myth and reality, perverse narcissists are not able to maintain friendships with men who are not in love with them; so they build formal relationships with people of the same sex (except for adoring "friends"), avoid men who represent a sort of "authority" and easily start fights with whomever they consider as threatening for their hegemony. After the adolescence period, the narcissist is often an isolated individual who looks for company by searching for a prey who can relieve his sense of social inadequacy and the inability to maintain stable and genuine relationships.

The myth of Echo and the end of Narcissus

The nymph Echo - desperate to the point of dying because of Narcissus' refusal - represents the portrait of the love addicted. Echo chases Narcissus through the woods and he, who was only interested in his reflection, ignores her: this causes a fatal suffering. Echo keeps being in love with Narcissus despite his refusal and, literally, dissolves in her own pain, becoming a voice in the woods. This nymph, desperately and stubbornly in love with Narcissus, has a lot of metaphorical features which take her closer to the love addicted psychology: she is a woman who forgets about herself, who gets lost in a meaningless sentiment, perhaps fed by the refusal and the impossibility of a reciprocity.

Furthermore, as frequently happens to love addicted, Echo comes from a past of exclusion and abuse. Ovid recounts that the nymph was noticed by Zeus because of her oratorical skills; the father of Gods asked her to distract his wife Juno by gossiping, so he could cheat on her with the mountain nymphs.
But Juno discovered it and inflicted a terrible punishment upon the nymph: she could not speak and was doomed to repeat the last word heard from her interlocutor forever.

If we considered Zeus and Juno as parents, Echo would be used by her father for his own purposes and against her mother. Zeus would be an unreliable, unfair, fickle father with an undisputed charm; Juno would be a strict mother whose relationship with her daughter changes according to her needs. These aspects are also frequent during the childhood of future love addicted. The Echo's inclination to gossip is also interesting because, considering a comparison with reality, a recurring characteristic in love addicted is the tendency to talk too much about what comes to their mind, to tell everything about other people as if they were not able to clearly draw their identity border lines without speaking about another subject.

The Echo's role adds some fascination to the myth of Narcissus, just like the love addicted does – more or less consciously; it feeds and magnifies the narcissist's sense of power. Echo destroys herself while Narcissus ignores and ridicules her by preferring his own reflection; the same way, those who suffer from love pains keep looking for a true relationship with their partner even when all evidences show that the same relationship will never work.

Narcissus died by drowning, Echo disappeared remaining alive somehow, trapped in a state of living death; she was doomed to eternally repeat the last syllables she heard. Also in reality, who experiences a love addiction, lives a very sad destiny: a loneliness crowded with specters, made of illusory love mirages and confused by conjectures.

The myth of Narcissus sounds like a warning and seems to tell us that the impossible love really is impossible. A simple message which went through centuries but does not reach our heads, nor can stop us from struggling against our weaknesses.

The narcissist's "recapture" strategies

It is so sweet to be loved,
that we are even happy with appearances.
(E. D'Houdetot)

The fear of being abandoned and replaced is among the most important features of the love addiction; it represents the main reason why those who suffer from it, cling to the love object with all their strength, beyond any evidence which shows the unstable and pathological essence of the relationship. So, the perverse narcissist relies on the partner's fear of being abandoned and betrayed, aware of the fact that the more his partner will feel inadequate, the more he will gain control of her life, satisfying his narcissistic needs. The "victim" of this love obsession sees her partner as powerful and desired, idealizes and glorifies him, not realizing she is dealing with a fragile person who is unable to give love; she can't imagine she is essential to her "oppressor". This is proved by the fact that, at the moment the partner breaks the addiction patterns, the perverse narcissist tries to recapture her with strategies aiming at recovering the relationship. This behavior totally surprises those who are experiencing a "detoxification" and can feed the love illusion. "If he comes back to me, it means he has forgiven me for all my unpleasant flaws", "Now everything is going to change and I will put all my efforts to make this relationship work": these are the things the "victim" tends to think. She ignores she is dramatically falling into the addiction again and months or years of useless suffering are waiting for her.

The narcissistic "recapture" strategies.

According to the perverse narcissist's logic, abandonment is unacceptable. The victim's escape is considered as a wound in his identity, an intolerable attack to his need of power and control of the partner. This causes - usually in an unconscious way - what the "victim" perceives as a sincere partner's return, but it basically is a trap. Analyzing tens of cases I've observed that narcissists always use the same recapture strategies. There is a disturbing repetitiveness in these behaviors and in the reaction of the prey who often falls into a trap: the macabre dance of love pains starts again.

The recapture strategies can reappear a few weeks after the end of the relationship or even after years.

In this sense, the "victim" can never let down her guard and must be aware that risks can arise again after long time, unless she has reached a new psychological and emotional balance that makes her immune from the narcissist's influence. But in this case, the ex-love addicted would not have any interest in his past "love".

The recapture strategies or "recapture plans" are four:

- the silence strategy;
- the guilt strategy;

- the flattery strategy;
- the symptom strategy.

The silence strategy

When the prey reacts against love addiction, exasperated by the pain, the perverse narcissist's first move is to remain still. He knows the victim, he knows she can't escape so easily; he imagines her getting more and more obsessed, crying and suffering to the point that she will then come back more "in love" than ever. Furthermore, the partner's attempt to escape allows the oppressor to have a break from a relationship which he felt as "too demanding", and to do the activity he likes the most without any obstacle: amusing himself. The perverse narcissist has an extremely broad time perception: if to his "victim", an hour is like a century, several weeks are nothing to him; for this reason he is an expert in the art of waiting, like a spider which delicately sleeps on its web.

The silence pattern is always the first choice. It doesn't cause suffering to the narcissist; on the contrary, it is a funny game which ends with the return of the sheep to the fold. While his partner suffers, the narcissist acts like a cold and detached reptile, able to survive without eating for weeks, extremely sure that silence is the best way to win and that it will make the victim weaker and more likely to be oppressed.

As an expert predator, the perverse narcissist knows well that his partner won't leave him without food: she will have a look to his Facebook page and send him indirect messages; when her level of despair will reach the highest peak, she will send him a text message or a paradoxical card in which she says: "You're not going to hear from me anymore!".

Then, if the silence strategy doesn't work, there is the plan B: the guilt strategy.

The guilt strategy

If the silence strategy doesn't work because of the prey's will to get out of the addiction trap, the perverse narcissist changes his strategy and opts for his favorite one which worked in the past. The guilt strategy is a clever mix of attacks, offences and insults aiming at destroying the partner's self-esteem and making her come back, pushed by the illusion of a narcissist's change. She can also be pushed by the despair of really considering herself as unpleasant and undesirable. So, there is no choice: she has to live a "love" made of unhappiness and oppression.

The perverse narcissist is an infallible archer and hits the crucial points of his prey: her physical appearance and sexuality ("You're fat", "You suck in bed, nobody wants you!"); values and morality ("She took advantage of my patience", "You're a w***e, I'm sure you're going to screw everybody"); family and friends (It's all your friend/mother/sister's fault if we are in this situation", "You hang out with that scum and you have really become like them!"). These are the three favorite targets which can cause an intense pain, a pain which stuns and impedes the victim to defend her own integrity and the decision to stop the massacre.

To carry out the guilt strategy, the narcissist mainly uses indirect channels, such as Facebook, Msn, online chats, since his mantra is "get the maximum result with minimum efforts". Then a series of accusations starts and pushes the addicted person to react and be available for explanations. If the online messages didn't cause the desired effects, there would also be other methods to attack. For example, by letting the victim know about a new sort of "liking" for someone else or directly creating a situation to vent all his own (narcissistic) disappointment on the "victim"… and that's it! The trap worked. The recapture has occurred.

The plan B fallibility is very low because – as absurd as it may seem – for the "victims", confirming the negative opinions they have of themselves represents a new and illusory occasion for redemption and to win their "real love" over again.

The flattery strategy

The perverse narcissist would design this trap if the previous two recapture strategies (silence and guilt) didn't work. This method consists of saying to the victim what she expects and would like to hear, giving her lots of compliments, talking about the love feeling she is hungry for, making her believe that the relationship will have a future. "I've got plans for us", "You're always on my mind", "You're special to me": phrases which well express the recapture based on flatteries. It is clear that it's not about poems or love declarations; very few narcissists go beyond some sweet and vague phrase, because for the addicted partner that's enough to make them feel love.

The flattery has the function to give the victim a new hope so to regain psychological control on her. Once the control has been regained, the perverse narcissist's self-esteem, compromised by the prey's attempt to escape, is immediately recovered, with the consequence to take the relationship back to the previous stage. The flattery strategy can be indirect or direct. The first technique, which is emotionally less "demanding", is the narcissist's favorite one and entails the use of social networks or text messages. For example, it takes just an oversentimental song to make the victim feel irrational nostalgia and tenderness… and that's it! The direct flattery, on the contrary, consists in giving the victim a little gift, sending some flowers or an unexpected dinner date, with the official intention to explain everything. In these cases, the perverse narcissist is expert in manipulating the discussion: as a result, the victim will fall into his trap.

Even if rarely, it can occur that the partner resists to the first flatteries because of their ambiguity. In these rare cases, the narcissist can even promise to change and talk about love… but then he comes back to act as he used to do.

If the flattery strategy fails, there are two options left: going back to insults or the final weapon, the ace in the hole, the symptom strategy.

The symptom strategy

If one of the previous strategies (silence, guilt and flattery) doesn't work, the perverse narcissist opts for another one and, in case of a new failure, chooses the third. Silences, blaming and flatteries can be used several times: the result is a nerve-wracking spiral of ambiguous behaviors which stun and recapture the prey.

It is just a matter of time: it usually takes a few weeks to wear out the victim's willpower and push her to come back. The narcissist is not in a hurry, unless he realizes that his strategies have been unveiled. After a repeated failure of the three basic recapture strategies, he could react with rage and pain, convincing his partner that he really loves her. "He really needs me and he doesn't know it, because he is afraid of love... But time will change him". This is the pathetic sign of defeat, the beginning of a nightmare which is worse than the previous one.

The stubborn and unstoppable escape of a no-more addicted partner brings chaos to the narcissist's emotional nature and makes him react childishly. Cries, incoherent explanations, object throwing, self-destructive actions and alcohol or substances abuse can precede the final attempt of narcissistic recapture: the symptom development. It is important to highlight that the narcissist really gets ill and, unconsciously uses his condition to attract the ex-partner. "I broke my leg", "Maybe I have a brain tumor", "I haven't been sleeping and eating for days, I don't know what's happening" are examples of symptoms.

They could also seem as stupid and childish psychological lures – according to an ordinary logic, they really are – but they work: the addicted partner thinks that she can't leave "the man she used to love" alone in so serious circumstances. This demonstrates that the psycho-logic regulates love addictions...

The symptom strategy represents the peak of the pathology. It is the extreme demonstration of the control need, the egoism and the affective mutilation the perverse narcissists and their victims are subject to.

The most difficult task for those who want to stop the addiction is to refuse the illusory possibility to really take care of the partner and put him aside with a healthy and aware egoism before he attacks again. At several levels, psychic and/or physical suffering traps people in a love addiction. They often see the perverse narcissist as a strict parent whose trust has to be regained or a depressed one to comfort with childish condescension.

Resisting to win

The first thing to do is to unveil the narcissist's strategies. It is painful but fundamental. What is your perverse narcissist doing? Which strategies does he use? Which trap would he use in case of failure? He is no longer a Prince Charming but a kamikaze loaded with TNT who sips a drink beside you, in your bed. What do you want to do? The violence of a psychological recapture through the symptom strategy in love addictions can reach unimaginable peaks and create solid bonds.

It is very hard to get out of this type of situations, since the partner's fragility, sadness and misery are based on different significant feelings: guilt sense, the need of being useful, the illusion of being appreciated; these are common feelings in the perverse narcissists' "victims". Getting out is possible only by regaining self-respect and defending it firmly, leaving the narcissist at the mercy of his mirror and monsters. Without Any Possibility of Appeal and Forever.

The female narcissist and manipulator

*Victims and oppressors feel the same disgust,
can be recognized from the same difficulties.*
(Laurent Mauvignier)

Pathological narcissism is not an exclusive male prerogative, but it can seem so in light of the stories told by lots of women subjugated by perverse narcissists. There are very few cases of female narcissism in the specialist literature: this seems to confirm the false belief that emotional manipulation is a men's prerogative.

This is partially due to the fact that the documented cases of narcissism mostly derive from clinical observation and the stories told by the "victims"; women are more apt to recount their affective stories to a therapist than men.

Usually, men involved in a sentimental addiction with a female narcissist prefer not to ask for help, according to sort of "code of honor"; therefore, they suffer for the dysfunctional relationship and also feel shame and guilt. These feelings make the female narcissists partially invisible, since their victims "cover" them by choosing silence.

The female narcissist and manipulator

The female equivalent of the perverse narcissist is a narcissist and manipulator: women, despite the differences with men, make their partner live the same hell made of abandonment, underestimation and humiliation.

The main features of the female narcissist are:

- illusion of being unique and grandiose;
- the belief of being special and knowing everything;
- the constant need of love displays and appreciation;
- envy;.

She is egocentric, lacks of the ability to properly interpret the other people's emotions and tends to see with a Machiavellian malice even the most genuine and clear behaviors.

A female pathological narcissist shows a clear tendency to feel persecuted; this leads to constant conflicts and causes the end of interpersonal relationships justified by blaming the others of being ungrateful and mean.

In love relationships, the female narcissist and manipulator initially behaves as a perverse narcissist. She's capable of surprising love displays and declarations and seems to be adoring and generous before starting with the following destructive phase. But there are no other analogies: the male narcissist becomes fickle and cold towards his partner while the female one starts an endless process in which she puts all her efforts to change her partner.

What keeps the relationship alive is the sense of inadequacy she makes the partner constantly feel: "You don't do enough for me",

"You should have told or done like this", "You're a useless man", "Real men don't behave like this" are the phrases a female narcissist say, always showing dissatisfaction. This disapproving attitude is also referred to his family, friends, job, the way he dresses and his salary. Everything is analyzed and manipulated by the female narcissist so to make her partner reach her level.

Coup de théâtre and psychological soap operas

Both partners end up isolating themselves from the outside world. They base their relationship on her unhappiness and his attempts to fulfill any of her requests so to avoid the extreme failure: the betrayal and the definitive end of the relationship. Actually, a relationship with a female narcissist and manipulator is made of constant fights and temporary interruptions which always end with reconciliations, even when it seemed to be really over. These returns have the same emotional intensity of a soap opera coupe de théâtre and can occur in two ways:

1- he begs for her to come back and promises to change; she forgives him unconditionally, showing the pureness of her love, but then she will make him pay for leaving or forcing her to leave him;

2- she is the one who asks him to come back after insulting and cursing him; she seems to be willing to change and maintain the relationship, but then she will make him pay for pushing her to humiliate herself.

In both cases, the relationship goes on always based on an impossible separation which leads to a partner's psychological consumption. Even when this consumption turns into a symptom, the partner doesn't give in. Insomnia, anxiety, difficulty in focusing, pathologic jealousy, sexual dysfunctions, alcohol or substance abuse are among the disorders which can appear in love addictions.

The relationship with a female narcissist and manipulator is most likely to end with an abandonment at the very moment in which the partner thinks he has fulfilled all her needs or, at least, has reached a sort of stability.

She leaves him for good and, in a really short period of time, starts a new relationship with her (next) "real love".

The intentionality enigma

*The unforgivable lie
is the one we told ourselves
with the only purpose to believe
to the other's falsehood, for love.*

The comments and e-mails on love addiction and pathological narcissism I receive every day are hundreds. Some of them recount really dramatic love stories; other talks about the importance of psychotherapy as a way to get rid of love pains and start to live again (see the Chapters "Stories"). But, what all these messages have in common is a question:

"Does the narcissist realize about the pain he causes? Is he aware of it? Does he act with intentional wickedness or is he an unaware sick person who acts following sick instincts?".

A psychological enigma.

I would call this question "the narcissistic intentionality enigma"; "enigma" because there is not an unambiguous answer, but above all, because any answer to this question leads to new problems and magnifies the victims' obsession for their lover. In fact, like all other psychopathologies, the love addiction is a sort of closed circuit which feeds itself and goes beyond rationality until it remains unchanged, even in front of the evidence and the logic. Some of the victims want to know they are dealing with a sane person, so to continue with the self-sacrifice and the self-destruction due to the inability to accept their sad relationship or even the end of it; others try to prove they are living with a sick person to try to cure him or convincing him to go to therapy so to make their love dream come true. From this perspective, whatever the answer is "Yes, he's sick" or "No, he isn't", the love addiction doesn't change, but it can even make the involvement grow.

However, although my answer to the enigma won't be therapeutic, I can say that the pathological narcissist is mostly unaware of the consequences caused by his behavior; even when it seems to be intentional and planned, it is the sign of a personality disorder.

Clinicians unanimously agree on a narcissistic fundamental trait: lack of empathy, which means the incapability to correctly interpret and feel the other people's emotions. This is sufficient to explain the reason why pathological narcissists show destructive behaviors without any sense of guilt, not realizing their ferocity in sentimental interactions.

What leads the love addicted to depression and self-annihilation is the attempt to explain - according to their empathic perspective - the reasons of their love drama, to rationalize their pains believing that they are dealing with a "sane" individual, often considered as more balanced and better than the other people. This "logical trap" leads to do everything to fulfill the narcissist's requests, hoping to win him over again.

No, the pathological narcissist doesn't act in this destructive way because of his partner's inadequacy. He does it because of his emotional disorders, which can be caused by an inner conflict remained unsolved; behind the grandiose appearance, he hides a childish Self full of rage and pain, prisoner from a long time and unable to love.

So, "victims", instead of asking themselves about the identity of the "monster" which oppresses them, could ask themselves in front of a mirror:

"Who am I? How can I save myself from this situation?" and start to "save themselves" to find a new balance, fulfilling their relational needs.

.

Is it possible to help the narcissist?

Cannot do without something or someone
doesn't mean that we own them,
but that we are owned.

Pain, anguish and confusion showed by those in a relationship with a perverse narcissist, are magnified by the impotence felt anytime they look for a change or a solution. Those who have experienced an "impossible relationship" know that submission and rebellion, together with reconciliations, are not good solutions. Armistices and "breaks", compromises and non-belligerence agreements sometimes can alleviate the pain or lead to those ecstatic moments which precede the harshest and devastating end. At the same time, showing the narcissist all the suffering he causes is useless: the result is a psychological execution, a threat of abandonment or even indifference and betrayal.

Like the nymph Echo, who in the myth of Narcissus was doomed to repeat her loved one's last words – in vain and endlessly -, the narcissist's partners seem to be trapped in a hard search for a way to get out of their narcissist's inner abyss to save him.

Only those who have an impossible relationship know how a narcissist can be intimately compromised at a psychological and emotional level. The fact that the partner is the only one to know about the pathology, clashes with the grandiose and credible appearance the narcissist shows to the outside world and also impedes any possibility to make a change in most part of the cases.

The narcissist refuses all types of help, he denies a profound inadequacy sense. At the same time, he distrusts everybody and often hates - openly or with an unconcealed fear – psychologists and psychotherapists. So, meeting the narcissist in a therapy session is only possible when - because of a personality disorder - depression, consequences of substance abuse, insomnia or other "collateral disorders" become unbearable. Because the clever narcissist only acts for himself, whenever or wherever he needs to take advantage of other people (therapist included).

As far as I know, after almost fifteen years of clinical experience, a narcissist will never say: "I'm here because I don't want to stay without my woman/man because of my behavior", or: "I need your help, Doctor, because even if I try to make it better, my relationship is impossible". This only happens in the victim's head. The idea that the narcissist will start a therapy and change for love is illusory and maintains the relationship alive; sometimes, it becomes an unrealistic objective, pursued until reaching the paradox which feeds the emotional addiction.

Very often, the narcissist's partners go to therapy not for themselves but to ask for "advices" on how to treat their partner, to help him/her and keep their love relationship alive, in spite of everything. They can also ask how to make the narcissist go to therapy.

In his lovers' fantasies, the narcissist will try to change, to be a better partner, starting a psychological path to maintain and "repair" the love relationship; he will eventually become more human and there will be a marriage, one or two kids and a happy life after a tough period… But it is impossible, actually.

The request for a change via other people is a symptom of a stubborn addiction, a detachment from reality the "victim" eventually experiences.

At the same time, the narcissist will keep belittleing, playing hide-and-seek, seducing and betraying in an evil and unstoppable series of goodbyes. Then, he will quickly find a new partner, he will have a baby and "camouflage" himself in a family, especially when - at a certain age - he needs a social "cover".

Even when getting married or pretending to be in a stable relationship, the narcissist escapes and, at the same time, "executes" his previous lovers, takes revenge on those who has continued to love him in spite of his pathology.

According to Behary (2012), generally narcissists are not that type of people who intentionally search for help, training or any type of support to tear down the walls of their emotional limits. On the contrary, they avoid this kind of interactions at all costs both by mocking, blaming someone else and through a firm refusal.

So, the narcissist cannot be pushed or forced to ask for help in any way, especially if the partner asks him to go to therapy.

However, the pathological narcissist hides a love nucleus, a "healthy" nucleus which can be reactivated with psychotherapy, on condition that he decides on his own to start this new path in an autonomous way, to face his limits and symptoms which push him towards unhappiness and frustration.

In this sense, psychoanalysis, psychodynamic psychotherapy, bioenergetic approach and Schema Therapy – just to mention some models – have defined specific treatments for the narcissistic personality disorder; for decades these disciplines have been working to support patients in dealing with their suffering, isolation and anguish deriving from narcissism.

All things considered, "victims" can only help narcissists by making them aware of the fact that their relationship confirms the narcissistic disorder. It is important that the narcissists' partners realize that their "sick" relationship is a consequence (not a cause) of a personality disorder and what they call "love" is actually a symptom or a psychopathology, not a feeling.

Helping the narcissist is a psychotherapeutic task, a specialist job which cannot be carried out by the "victim" within the addiction relationship.

The love addiction

... but I was afflicted by torment,
afflicted by the loss of you.
(Alda Merini)

One night, Licia lost control of herself. She wore a coat over her pajamas and got in her car at two o'clock in the morning. She absolutely had to go to Francesco's house. Even if she knew she wouldn't have had the guts to ring the doorbell and talk to him, even if she knew their shutters would have been closed, she felt that she had to go there. So, she drove with tears in her eyes and parked the car without any care. Once she turned the car off, for a moment, she did the same with her heart. As soon as she got there, just the sight of his house door made her calm down and alleviated the anguish of losing him; she suddenly stopped crying. She felt a big hole in her mind. In those apparently quite moments, Licia realized how that situation was absurd; she reproached herself and promised not to tell it to anybody. She felt a deep shame and, while she was trying to put herself together, her own reflection in the rearview mirror made her sad.

How did she end up like this? And, above all, why? The fact that Francesco had left her a few months before didn't justify the anxiety and depression she was suffering from and that were getting worse day after day. In a moment of lucidity she admitted that their relationship was insignificant, that things went wrong since the beginning and she forced herself to stay with him, pushed by the desire of having a relationship.

He left her without a reason, sure, but deep down then she thought it was better to break up; it was just a matter of weeks or months before she would have made this decision. He, who seemed to be the man of her dreams, was a complete disaster. Francesco was egoist, egocentric, narcissist and, a part from a few Hollywood-style phrases, he lacked of empathy. In bed he was a disaster: in one year of relationship, Licia had never reached an orgasm. "What am I doing in front of that idiot's house?" Licia told herself as soon as the anguish totally stopped. But then, she started thinking too much again, without a reason. She started thinking that Francesco was sleeping with another girl, so the anxiety she felt was about to take her breath away.

Mental blackout. For her, it was difficult trying not to get off the car and ring the doorbell. But she decided to remain there until the morning to see if Francesco already had a new girlfriend: she would have seen her going out of the apartment. That thought destroyed Licia and made her cry violently again.

From that night on, Licia went in front of Francesco's house for a few weeks. She did it more times a day. She always checked if he was home alone and this calmed her down in the same way that the sight of his windows alleviated her anxiety. There was nothing left which could help her; she passed the days obsessed. When he realized that Licia was spying on him, he reported it to the police. It was the most humiliating moment of her life, but also the moment in which she decided to go to therapy to save herself from a love addiction.

Impulsiveness, mood swings and asymmetric relationships

Licia's story shows three useful features to identify a pathological love relationship: impulsiveness, mood swings and asymmetric roles within the relationship. Those who suffer from a love addiction experience these three dynamics in several combinations and different intensity, before they turn into clinical symptoms usually connected to relationship addictions, such as anxiety, panic attacks, depression and eating disorders.

Impulsiveness is the inability to contain our own impulses, especially towards our love object; it comes from the need to have "all and now": the impulse cannot be postponed, waiting is impossible and painful therefore, it takes to act immediately. The love addicted now can no longer tolerate frustrating emotions and acts by doing the first thing which can keep the anguish away from her, even if, at a rational level, she is perfectly aware that it will be useless and counterproductive. For example, while Licia was driving to Francesco's, she was perfectly aware it was useless but, at the same time, the impulse dominated her.

In Licia's story, it is clear how her mood swings from anguish to moments of extreme lucidity, and eventually to a total confusion. This feature is common in people who experience a dysfunctional relationship. The quick change from despair to excitement and then to total confusion causes a mood instability which eventually influences all the aspects of a person's life and leads to a pathology.

Licia lost her enthusiasm at work, became fickle and aggressive; looking for comprehension from her colleagues worsened her conditions. As usually occurs, her confidences caused a series of opinions, judgments and advices which made her level of frustration – and her mood instability – grow.

Mood swings, generally in a depressive sense, are among the main reasons which feed the love addiction. The partner, with his emotions, behaviors and reactions, gradually becomes the only person able to alleviate the pain. His presence reduces the pain of refusal and loneliness, even if, at the same time, magnifies the sense of uselessness and abandonment.

So, each addiction is the result of a drastically unbalanced pathological relationship in terms of esteem, power, give and take.

Every addiction grows within an asymmetric relationship in which a member of the couple prevails and the other one is subjugated. The asymmetric relationship entails the existence of differences between what the partners can do, ask for and give; the more the relationship gets pathological, the less it is mutual. Licia was subjugated by Francesco's needs. She had to live according to his life and tolerate his silences. And this was the least. Francesco had the right to ask her about her sexual and emotional life, while Licia wasn't allowed to do it. Francesco could decide if and how to meet her, Licia's role was to wait. A total lack of reciprocity makes the relationship asymmetric and pathologic.

Impulsiveness, mood instability and asymmetry are a toxic mix which can transform people into love addicted, in a person who has no longer control of his life and shows "unexplainable" and always more serious symptoms destined to build a love prison.

Thoughts, emotions and behaviors

All psychological disorders act on three levels: thoughts, emotions and behaviors. In love addictions, each of these features is subject to specific alterations which permit to distinguish the syndrome from other psychopathologies, such as depression, anxiety and panic attacks. However, it is necessary to highlight the difficulty in reaching a differential diagnosis, especially because depression, anxiety and panic attacks, obsessions and somatization generally appear with love addictions. Therefore, it takes to ask ourselves whether these disorders cause the love addiction or they represent its consequences.

Actually, if we exclude a personality disorder diagnosis, searching for "causes" and "consequences" within the clinical practice is counterproductive as well as useless.

First of all, the Love Addiction is the result of an interactive process, the quality of a relationship between two individuals which triggers vicious circles made of actions and reactions within an endless game. The love addiction cannot be exclusively considered as an individual-related disorder: it is proved by the fact that therapists frequently deal with patients who have never suffered from psychological disorders in the past and at the beginning of the relationship were serene; then, they fell in a hell made of obsessive thoughts and despairing emotions. This means that, from a therapeutic perspective, searching for "causes" related to the individual and his or her past can be misleading: it can lead to analyze the past, ignoring the "here and now", the present in which the disorder grows.

A fundamental assumption of strategic psychotherapy and psychology, theorized by Watzlawick and Nardone (1990), says that if a problem persists in the present, it means that behaviors, emotions and thoughts are ongoing in the same present and feed the pathology day after day.

Assuming that the problem comes from a remote past, it is necessary to observe that its growth is strictly related to the present.

An unambiguous definition of Love Addiction doesn't exist, also because it is a pathology caused by interactive patterns which can also be very different. Each love addiction story, besides having common psychopathological features, is an independent case and needs to be dealt with by starting a "personalized" therapy for and with the patient.

To study the Love Addictions, it is necessary to find a definition of the investigation scope, also including the highest number of variations the problem can show.

A definition of Love Addiction

The Love Addiction is a disorder of the emotional and relational sphere, characterized by the importance of a "love object" the addicted subject has dysfunctional feelings of exclusivity for.

The Love Addiction progressively influences the cognitive, emotional and behavioral levels of people who suffer from it, and leads to a disorder which symptoms are recognizable. These symptoms lead to a significant worsening in the different areas of the patient's everyday life; it can cause a serious damage of a person's general functioning.

Similarly to other addictions, the Love Addiction gradually appears in a context of "normality". Changes of thoughts, emotions and behaviors first appear as isolated episodes and then lead to a real clinical syndrome.

Cognitive features

The love addicted gradually develops an egocentric way of thinking, which leads her/him to consider herself/himself as the cause of her/his love object's behaviors. This way of thinking transforms clear signals of abandonment into a confused but captivating proof of love; chance gestures such as messages of interest and sexual seduction. The meaning of words in a love addiction makes the reality perception change. The result is that the love addicted feels as if he/she lives in a world he/she doesn't understand, in which he/she doesn't feel understood; his/her attempts to make him/her "open his or her eyes" on the evidence of the relational pathology turn into hostility. Lots of love addicted lose most of their friends and maintain those who don't criticize their love "choices".

The main traits of the way of thinking in a love addiction are:

- a constant attention on the love object;
- tendency to consider ourselves and/or the relationship as the cause of the partner's behaviors;
- obsessive thoughts;

- tendency to overestimate the positive signals and underestimate the opposite ones;
- difficulty in concentration;
- idealization of the love object;
- other types of relationships are considered as obstacles or threats to the love relationship.

Emotional features

In love addiction a person goes from happiness and passion to refusal, rage and despair in few days and, sometimes, hours. This particular emotional swing frequently causes cyclothymia, bipolar depression and a huge series of personality disorders.

In love addictions, emotions are at the service of the relationship. So, since the same relationship is characterized by serious inconsistencies, ambiguity and discontinuity, the emotional state of at least one of the two partners constantly changes.

Some of the characteristics of the emotions felt within a love addiction are:

- anxiety and a sensation of alert or imminent danger;
- a rather depressed mood with agitation peaks;
- tendency to attribute our own emotions to the love object (Projection);
- rage burst associated with loss of self-control are likely to occur;

- abandonment and loneliness felt even in presence of significant people:
- Sense of void and lack of meaning;
- progressive emotional detachment from the outside world and social self-isolation;
- emotions always focused on the love object.

Behavioral features

The "visible" part of the love addiction refers to behaviors, which progressively become more pathological.

The addictive behaviors, characterized by quick and harsh changes, gradually develop.

The actions of the people involved express happiness and passion which suddenly turn into rage and despair; they're not controlled.

The individual is overwhelmed by his or her own impulses and dominated by the need to convert them into acts, even when, at a rational level, the same is able to understand that they are useless and pathological.

This is a brief list of behavioral features in love addictions:

- Compulsive behaviors: repeated and uncontrolled actions such as phone calls, e-mails and text messages sending;
- submissive attitude towards the love object: we get along with the partner's wishes so to have his or her attention;
- incapability of making decisions;
- tendency to delegate our own responsibilities;

- tendency to miss appointments or important activities so to see our partner;
- a constant waiting status;
- investigation or tailing attempts to create an "illusion of control" on the love object..

Clinical features

The progressive change of our way of thinking, emotions and behaviors creates and feeds vicious circles, action and responses patterns which make the disorder grow until it turns into pathology. This negative situation becomes systematic and then is transferred from the love relationship to other significant relationships and contexts.

As we will see in the following chapters, the Love Addiction symptoms attack the main functions of the human being and his basic needs: food, rest, sociability.

The six phases of love addiction

*A first initial mistake is sufficient
to make all things wrong.*
(Alessandro Morandotti)

While I was listening to Mrs. B.'s story, I kept imaging her going down a gloomy and bare staircase which led to solitude, anxiety, panic, obsession and depression. It took ten months of relationship with Armando - a man she met at work - to transform Mrs. B. into a distressed and sleepless robot, constantly searching for love. Smart, strong and good-looking forty-year-old businesswoman, Francesca B. boasted a great emotional balance. She had never showed any particular symptom or trauma. Insomnia, anxiety, lack of appetite and an obsession with the man who had left her without any explanation were new experiences for her. She asked me and herself: "How is it possible that I ended up like this?". Francesca B.'s story follows a pattern which is similar to those of other relationships turned into love addictions. After a few days of uncontrollable passion, the relationship with Armando slowed down; he became fickle and, two months later, he suddenly left her without any reason. Then, after sleepless nights, chases and despaired pleas, Francesca lost control on her life and spent entire days waiting for a sign from

Armando or any news about him from some of their common friends.

"It's as if you went down the stairs of a psychological addiction to Armando", I say.

Francesca answered: "Doctor, I feel as if I had taken an elevator which went down to hell".

The elevator metaphor struck me because it describes the love addiction dynamics: not a slow and gradual process, as the staircase metaphor suggests, but a fall from a pain to another just like the elevator moves from a floor to another one. At first we are at the ground floor, then 100 feet underground. This characteristic makes the love addiction very dangerous, since the subjects involved don't have enough time to realize about the pathogenic nature of the relationship; they are surprised by such sudden and unexpected changes. For example, during a specific phase, the people they love seem to appreciate them, almost living according to their partners' needs. Then, suddenly, they despise their partners.

At first, the partner is generous and attentive then he unexpectedly turns into a cruel enemy, an intransigent inquisitor or a fleeting ghost.

Which are the phases of a love addiction? It is possible to describe the addicted people's fall? Although each story is different from the other ones - characterized by behaviors, thoughts and emotions which cannot be generically described - clinical cases have shown a series of common phases which follow one another just like the floors of a building. Each phase represents the basis for the following one and the passage from one to another is very quick, as if the floors of the building were always more frightening and painful. The last floor of love addiction is the symptom development: depression, obsession, anxiety and panic or "physical" disorders which seem not to be related to the addicted person's past (from dermatological problems to reproductive, respiratory and digestive system dysfunctions).

The phases of love addiction

Within the research and intervention model for love addictions, developed by starting from the psychotherapy with tens of people (both male and female), I have identified six phases of the syndrome development. According to the same metaphor, in the psychological elevator of love addiction there are six buttons:

- Phase 1. First encounter: getting to know each other
- Phase 2. Ambivalence.
- Phase 3. Self-deception.
- Phase 4. Idealization.
- Phase 5. Active addiction.
- Phase 6. Actual symptomatic phase.

Phase 1. First encounter: getting to know each other

The love addiction syndrome generally starts to grow from simple encounters. The first contact occurs in a very normal way: through common friends, at the pizzeria, at the disco, on the Internet, maybe in a chat room. At least one of the potential partners feels the need of having a relationship; this need will play a crucial role while going down towards the following floors.

This phase usually causes bland feelings and goes on without particular episodes. According to the patients' stories, the person they become addicted to, at first seemed to be more interested in getting to know the potential partner. Generally, a love addiction starts without thinking about the consequences; the people involved believe it's just a pastime while waiting for real love.

Phase 2. Ambivalence

The almost insignificant impression of the first encounter remains during the following dates while the involvement level grows. Although the doubts still persist, they meet always more frequently; they spend always more time together and share always more things.

At this phase, one or both partners have doubts on continuing with the relationship. At some level, they clearly know that "he/she is not the right person", but is the only one who can comfort him or her.

A typical attempt to solve the ambivalence is to deny it, acting as if didn't exist; or by going on with the relationship so to dispel all doubts.

Such "solution" - which consists in leaving more freedom to the other or making more requests to him or her - causes confusion. For example, a classical turning point is the moment of the first sexual intercourse. Some patients reported they decided to do it so to dispel all doubts and resolve the ambivalence. In some cases, this has led to a sense of guilt due to the idea of taking advantage of the partner; in other cases to the need to "try again to understand something more"; in other cases to gratitude: the other person has been generous in spite of the ambiguity and the lack of involvement showed.

It is clear that these three possible results are not only extremely likely to occur but they all also lead to the same consequence: the relationship continuation.

During this second phase, violent discussions or fights can happen. These are the first symptoms of a discrepancy between conscious feelings (the acceptance of staying with the partner) and hidden emotions, relegated in an unconscious state, since they're inconvenient (the relationship is actually unsatisfying, frustrating or dangerous for his or her own integrity).

Phase 3. Self-deception

At this point, the level of involvement is so high that the ambivalence created needs to be solved. The solution is the self-deception. To stay with a partner who makes us feel opposite and indefinite emotions, it takes to project on him our emotional needs and pretend that he will be able to satisfy them, sooner or later.

Self-deception consists in telling ourselves "It doesn't matter if...". For example, it doesn't matter if the partner is selfish in bed or if there is no sexual harmony; it doesn't matter if he's not so generous; it doesn't matter if I get so bored with him; it doesn't matter if none of my friends likes him and so on. The unconscious objective of the addicted person is to remove any possible obstacle towards the dream of love. The self-deception can occur at different levels of depth, but lots of patients said they were at least partially aware during this phase. In people with love addiction, the need to have a partner, the fear of being lonely, the need to satisfy his or her relatives' and friends' expectations are so intense that they distort reality, transforming a dysfunctional relationship into an apparently satisfying one.

Since self-deception cannot completely hide the inadequacy of the relationship, the love addicted avoids the outside world reality and opts for staying alone with his partner.

By reducing the meetings with friends and other people, the narcissist also reduces the possibility of a confrontation with the outside world, therefore, the relationship is more likely to continue for long time.

The resulting gradual isolation will feed the addiction to the love object.

Phase 4. Idealization

Idealization is the direct consequence of self-deception and, from an emotional perspective, causes something which is similar to love. The previous phase function was to eliminate inconsistencies and flaws; this phase has the purpose to magnify or invent qualities to justify the relationship.

The partner seems beautiful, almost perfect and essential. Even the features that were considered as flaws before, at this point turn into positive qualities in the eyes of the love addicted. A progressive detachment from reality occurs: this gives the pleasant sensation to live suspended in a love relationship which flies above all and everything. Idealization can be very satisfying for the partner who, therefore, takes part with complicity in the creation of a distorted self-portrait, which partially matches with the partner's expectations.

In other cases, on the contrary, idealization is the beginning of the end of the relationship (but not the end of the addiction) since it frightens the love object and pushes him to go away from the addicted partner: he knows that he cannot satisfy the partner's great expectations.

Whatever the partner's reaction is, with this phase, the metaphorical descending elevator of love addiction has passed the middle line of its journey towards the disease and can hardly be stopped. The feelings towards the love object are solid, the partner is constantly focused on how to satisfy his desires.

During the idealization, everything is brought to the limit: too many text messages, phone calls, presents, plans. The love addicted constantly talks about her story, updates her friends, relatives and acquaintances on her relationship. In such cases —

which are numerous – at this stage, the partner decides to interrupt the relationship; so, the idealization process accelerates. The partner becomes irreplaceable because of his "escape"; so, the addicted person will have to bow down before him to make him come back. Or: the partner escapes because he's frightened by the depth and the sweetness of the feelings they have been sharing from the beginning; he escapes "because he's so in love with me and afraid of love". For this reason it will be necessary to help him to freely experience the beauty of the feelings they have discovered together. Those who experience these emotions really feel as if they were in love. Now, they are unable to distinguish reality from what they wanted to invent.

Phase 5. Active addiction

During the active addiction, the addicted partner focuses on the love relationship and changes her own life according to her partner's needs and expectations.

In this phase, the most significant symptoms are: gradual social isolation and mood swings, from euphoria to depression with a slight (or moderate) state of anxiety. Generally, during this phase, the addicted person's decisions and behaviors are totally based on the partner: these behaviors will affect her own existence and therapeutic path.

Some of the addicted partners, stops seeing her friends; others ask for a working hours reduction or save always more money to guarantee a stable future to the couple. The addicted subject, during this phase, seems to lose her control, floating in a "background world" filled with love dreams and the possibility of abandonment. Obviously, the addicted individual is unaware of what's happening and is more likely to violently refuse to be helped. So now, a situation of extreme fragility takes shape; in this condition any type of event can cause pain and make the psychic suffering more serious. The active addiction period can last weeks, months or years. Its duration also depends on the love object's actions, not on the addicted partner's decisions. The addicted partner is a "reactive subject", able to react but not to act in an autonomous way. Without a psychotherapeutic intervention, the active addiction persists if the partner doesn't decide to put less effort in the relationship or to interrupt it for any reason.

It is not rare that at some point, the emotional costs of the addiction exceed the advantages and the less involved subject, for this reason, decides to go away. At this point, the love addiction pathology is ready to explode with all its serious consequences. The elevator has almost finished its vertical journey to the center of hell.

Phase 6. Actual symptomatic phase

During the last phase, all the light symptoms which have previously appeared – alleviated by the apparent advantages of the relationship – are now more intense. The obsessive attention towards the love object is subject to a further alteration: a more definitive detachment from reality occurs. This is not surprising;

it is as if the world was six floors above the partner trapped into the depths of the love addiction. The world is very far and not so important. This is a dimension where enemies who don't understand "what love is" live; a place in which there is nothing to live for.

It is common to believe that the symptomatic phase occurs in solitude conditions, which means when the partner interrupts the relationship. Actually, the symptoms development does not depend on the partner's presence or absence, since the love addiction has a paradoxical logic in which any action made within the relationship results to be "wrong" and feeds the pathology. If the other one escapes, the desperation due to the abandonment causes a chase and a potentially endless series of refusals which makes the symptoms more serious. If the partner remains and accepts the relationship, the addiction grows and goes on: the addicted subject will repeatedly ask for more attentions until the relationship will collapse under the weight of its own dysfunctional nature.

The most significant clinical features are:

- Sleep disorders.
- Significant change in the food habits.
- Impulsiveness.
- Generalized anxiety with or without panic attacks.
- Compulsive use of mobile phones and/or Internet.
- Absence of social life.
- Sense of reality loss, from light to serious.
- Fragmented perception of the Self.
- Fear of losing control.

- Fear of going mad.
- Compulsive behavior.

How to intervene? How to save ourselves? At this point, the solution can be a psychotherapy aiming at helping the addicted person during the change process and understanding the strategies which have fed the addiction. Other symptomatic events, such as the psychiatric drugs consumption, which don't affect the perceptive-responsive system— emotions, thoughts and behaviors which rule his or her interaction with reality – in a significant way, rarely lead to a real change and escape from the love addiction labyrinth.

Love addiction and homosexuality

All love relationships are equal, although they seem to be really different; it takes to underline that "heterosexual" and "homosexual" love relationships can go off the rails and lead to a love addiction in the same way, with the same patterns and the same pain. Love is not about sexual orientation: love, even if crazy and sick, transcends the differences.

The pioneer of love addiction studies and psychotherapy, Robin Noorwood (1974) underlined that love pains are not an exclusive heterosexual prerogative and in same-sex relationships, they can be a further obstacle towards self-fulfillment, which is already complicated by a hetero-centric education and negative stereotypes on homosexuality.

Although psychological researches continue to demonstrate the opposite thesis (Rigliano, Gaglia, 2006), the belief that gays and lesbians have a promiscuous and unstable life can lead homosexuals to stubbornly continue with a dysfunctional relationship, with the implicit and socially shared belief that there are no alternatives. In fact, if heterosexuals can take stable love relationships as a reference, young homosexuals grow up with the absence of positive references of love between couples of men or women.

For the most fragile individuals, this hurtful emptiness experienced during the adult age is likely to lead to difficulties or disorders in the love and/or sexual sphere. Some of them can unconsciously conform to the prevailing stereotype, becoming sexually promiscuous and emotionally elusive; others can refuse such stereotype and live a solitary and sentimentally impenetrable life or follow the "right" model with a consequent marriage.

Other homosexuals, though, find the way to fight the stereotype of the impossible gay relationship, work on self-acceptance and search for a sentimental life which corresponds to their own actual emotional needs; they look for complicity, devotion, intimacy and stability. Obviously, this search can lead to stable and satisfying, stable but conflicting or unstable and unsatisfying gay relationships; or even to impossible relationships, such as those between heterosexuals.

Love addiction in homosexual relationships is not different from the nerve-racking swing of events, pauses and lies, infidelities and useless promises of the more classical heterosexual relationships.

Contrary to the heterosexual addicted, gay or lesbian addicted sees the decay of a dysfunctional relationship as the fulfillment of a familiar and cultural prophecy which condemns him or her to unhappiness and solitude; he or she feels the pain of a sick relationship and sees it as a personal failure, a ridiculous and "inevitable" result of his or her own incapability to love.

This pushes lots of homosexual addicted people to obsessively continue with unhappy, punitive and asymmetric relationships: the stereotype which considers gay love as troubled and tragic could lead a gay person to fall in the love addiction trap. When will a serious relationship happen again? Is he likely to experience a satisfying and balanced love relationship? Especially now that he's surrounded by the discouraging suggestions of a pessimistic love education.

According to the dark and incomplete representation internalized by the gay love addicted, a love relationship – even the most chaotic and scatterbrained ones – is a salvation from solitude and is worth a self-sacrifice.

Love addiction in couples of men or women can be darker and dangerous than in heterosexual couples. Social fabric, culture, family values and work relationships rarely push a person in an unhappy gay relationship to consider new perspectives and a sentimentally happy future. So, that solitude felt with the partner - typical of love pains both in heterosexual and homosexual relationships – can easily reach the edge of despair and lead to a deep psychological impasse.

Furthermore, a search for a psychological help is generally lived with more fear and skepticism than in heterosexual people. The gay couples' fear of not being accepted or being judged and considered as sick also in psychotherapy can inhibit help requests and convince the love addicted to cope with the problem and suffer on his own.

Actually, when love addiction affects a person's psychological life and causes a clinical disorder, a specific psychotherapy path can help in overcoming a crisis and support in reaching a new balance, whatever the relationship is gay or heterosexual. In love, we really are all equal.

Brief focal psychotherapy on love addictions

What leads to the solution of a psychological problem
is not the search for causes nor the interpretation of the consequences,
but the interruption of a relationship which joins
causes and consequences in a vicious circle
which makes the past current, in the present and in the future.

Carla thought Giacomo was the man of her life, the solution to a wrong marriage, the unexpected salvation come from an accidental encounter. That enigmatic and successful man could make her happy after an unhappy marriage; so, Carla became impulsive and impetuous as never before. She put her moral values aside together with her uncertainties and taboos of a strict sexual education.

Giacomo took everything. There was even no need to ask, since Carla didn't leave him the time to do it. She completely offered herself to him - anticipating all his needs - and was totally under his thumb. When depression showed her the evidence of a sick love, of a love addiction, it was too late to get out of it on her own. However, the reason which pushed her to go to therapy was to alleviate the symptoms, not to get rid of Giacomo; she just wanted to keep being his victim again and again. Then, when she started to feel better, despite knowing the pathological addiction mechanisms and that a relationship interruption was the only solution, Carla used her new energies and (temporary) balance to meet Giacomo again. She obviously found a childish and selfish man, an inquisitor; as a result, she started suffering again.

There is a limit of effectiveness in psychotherapy for any type of pathological addiction, love and relational addictions included. This limit is represented by our will to radically free ourselves from the addiction object, to abandon the vicious circles of a dysfunctional relationship. If the addicted person refuses to face an abstinence period, aiming at the total separation from the addiction object, the path towards change stops and can gradually lead back to the symptom, which sometimes is more serious than before. As well as in drug addiction therapy, it is necessary for the patient to stop the drug consumption so that the concepts acquired during the sessions can turn into awareness and lead to a stable change; in the same way, during the therapy for the love addiction, the patient have to recognize a "detoxification" period as necessary; he or she has to stay away from the partner to successfully finish the therapy.

In the brief therapy for relational addictions, I have identified a seven-step path; these steps have to be made in a specific order so that the intervention reach its goal: not only the radical annihilation of specific symptoms, but also the reconstruction of an identity which permits to live outside and beyond the pathological relationship.

The path consists of six moments which I will describe in the next paragraphs:

- Phase 0. First Session
- Phase 1. Insight Phase
- Phase 2. Latency Phase
- Phase 3. Implementation or active abstinence
- Phase 4. Corrective emotional experience
- Phase 5. Awareness Phase
- Phase 6. Consolidation.

Psychotherapy objectives

Although it is impossible to generalize or standardize objectives and time of the psychotherapy – because of the risk of depersonalization – the potentially infinite variety of cases can be included in seven big areas-objectives which are useful to analyze, together with the patient, mid-term and long-term objectives.

These areas-objectives identify the fields in which, often unconsciously, the person lacks because of his past and current relationship with himself or herself, the others and the outside world.

These are the seven areas-objectives:

Independence, the ability of making decisions according to our love needs and developing a sense of integrity and independence from the others' judgments and influence.

Self-esteem, it can be synthetically defined as the attitude of self-appreciation and self-acceptance through the integration of "positive" and "negative" aspects of the Self.

Self-realization, which refers to the tendency to use our own resources to express our potential and skills, also within our working environment.

Self-awareness, consists in "looking at ourselves within the relationship", which means the ability to identify our own emotional, cognitive and relational mechanisms, and recognizing the consequences of our behaviors and the quality of our communication with others and vice versa, in a flexible and dynamic way.

Assertiveness, the ability to communicate in an effective and constructive way, without being aggressive or submissive.

Open-mindedness, the tendency to genuinely talk and listen to other people, the will to make new friends, curiosity and trust in the neighbor.

Affection, is the area in which present and past of significant relationships meet, which contains - often unconsciously - the dysfunctional relationship patterns at the basis of the issues discussed during the sessions.

Phase 0. First Session

The first session with the psychotherapist generally causes expectations and anxiety. Independently of the problem the patient wants to talk about, he or she comes to the office after long reflections; usually a patient comes after several attempts to face his or her problem. The feeling which better describes the first approach to the therapy, especially in case of a love addiction, is "ambivalence"; a desire to share and the need to hide, a hope for a change and the skepticism towards the therapy; the need to free ourselves turns into fear of doing it in an inner dance which confuses and wear us out.

The strategic therapist considers the first appointment as a counseling session and acts as if it was the last one; so, he deals with the problem (with a suggestion, an interpretation of the disorder dynamics, the proposal of a psychotherapy path etc.) during that very session. For this reason, the psychotherapist listens to the person's story without saying anything, accepts tears and hesitations, asks questions to deeply understand, not judging the individual according to some standard theory. The patient – who faces a life full of fears and secrets – surprisingly feels that someone, the therapist, is facing life with him or her. It is the first important step towards the solution.

In case of a love addiction, a request for help is never unambiguous and rarely clear. The person asks for advices because he or she lives with an intolerable problem, but it is rare that he or she clearly recognizes the causes and shows a clear will to change. So, during session 0, it is necessary for the therapist to support the patient in openly talk about his or her problem and setting the goals which have to be reached as soon as possible (generally in 10-20 sessions).

At the end of the first session, the patients talk about a mix of "lightheartedness" and "fear". On one hand they really feel as they were able to break the chains with the help of psychotherapy; on the other hand, they focus on the hidden obstacles of the change process. In some cases they try to foresee the violent reactions of their partner to their "healing"; in other cases they imagine themselves as deprived of their "love drug", the subject they depend on, and this is something that they don't like at all at the moment of the first meeting.

Phase1. Insight Phase

The first phase of the therapeutic process focuses on how the problem "works". How does it appear? Which are its symptoms? Which consequences does it cause on the daily routine? Which are the thoughts, emotions and behaviors which feed it? Which are the ones that inhibit it?

Now, the focus is on the current features of the addiction and not on the patient's past. Encouraging the patient to carry out a detailed "archaeological" research on his or her own past could not allow him or her to find an effective solution and makes the number of therapy sessions increase.

From the strategic psychotherapy perspective, problems and solutions have to be found in the present and there isn't any reason to search for them in a remote "there and then", such as in traumatic events experienced as a child. Furthermore, it is useful to know that focusing on past experiences could be the perfect way for the patient not to analyze the present, the experiences he or she sees as big problems: this leads to a change postponement.

The patients who show a higher level of addiction tend to idealize their love object to such an extent that they don't blame him or her at all for their suffering. The partner is considered as "completely good", the patient has all responsibilities and – especially during the first sessions – makes a long list of self-accusations. "Maybe I should have told this...", "Maybe I made a mistake...", "Maybe I'm too demanding..." and so on. By blaming himself or herself for everything, the addicted person maintains the illusion of controlling the relationship: in fact, if the "relationship failure" is totally attributable to him or her, then a change will be enough to get the love relationship he or she desires.

This logic – which is apparently comforting – precedes a worsening of the pathology. Each attempt of "recapture" seems to intensify the anguish, the constant sense of alert and the transitory nature which characterizes the pathological addiction.

As we will see later, the most complex aspect in dealing with love addictions is helping the patient to realize that for as much as he or she can change according to the partner's needs, the situation won't change: an emotional desert where it is impossible for lilies to grow.

During the first phase of psychotherapy, the patient starts to know how his or her addiction works and which consequences it causes; he or she starts to notice that the remarks made during the sessions are true and "magically" predictive about what happens between the sessions.

These insights, generally, don't have the power of a solid awareness – which will be reached at a later stage – but, strategically speaking, it is good: it is the raindrop which digs in the rock and breaks the mountain.

The main function of the insight phase is to support the patient in improving an attitude which he or she lacks: the insight, which means the tendency to "foresee" his or her own reactions to the partner's actions, according to an unconscious process. A lot of love addiction cases seem to start and go on through an escalation of despair and pathology, since one of the subjects involved has decided to put himself or herself aside just "to live a love"...

Phase 2. Latency phase

At this stage of the therapeutic path, the initial symptoms have generally disappeared or diminished. For the patient, this is a moment of enthusiasm and hope. The enthusiasm comes from the fact that the therapy shows its benefits and diminishes anxiety and depression; the hope derives from the fact that the patient eventually feels as if he or she can change the situation and find a new balance. At this point, there is an increase of awareness and insights on how love addiction works, since reality confirms what has been foreseen during the sessions. Even though the person has "changed" and behaves differently with the object of the addiction, he or she tends to act the same way as before. What happens during the latency phase is that the answers from the partner - which the patient used to long for – now are felt as frustrating. Phone calls, encounters, text messages, "disappearances" and "returns", which still persist just like at the beginning of the therapy, have a new meaning: they are mechanical, predictable and unpleasant events. So, the patient gradually and slightly starts to reduce his or her degree of addiction; we are now dealing with latent emotions. The emotional reference is no longer the partner who tends to underestimate these changes. The fact that any contact with the partner is perceived as unpleasant is paradoxically considered as a problem. "I don't feel what I used to do", "At a certain point I can't wait to go away", "I was tempted not to answer the phone", the patients say during the latency phase, showing a veiled sorrow. In fact, now that even seeing the partner becomes unpleasant, which are the positive aspects of this relationship? What about now? Why does the pursuit have to go on?

During this phase, all the insights are combined with the emotional change and produce a further break in the patient's perceptive-responsive system: the addiction results to be weakened.

Though, during the latency phase, the patient often tends to use his or her new energy and wellness to go on with the relationship, convinced that, now that he or she feels stronger, it is possible to manage the relationship in a different way and make the partner change. This illusion during the latency phase is the same he or she experienced at the beginning of the therapy: if I change, improve, my partner will fall in love with me and everything will be fine. This utopia will cause serious effects on the patient at the end of the latency phase; in this phase, in fact, serious relapses are frequent: it can be explained by the collapse of the unconscious hope of a renewed and satisfying relationship under the weight of the evidences mentioned during phase 2.

The latency phase constitutes a crucial moment for the success of the psychotherapeutic path since it exposes the patient to frustration; the therapist has to show a higher ability of stress management and containment. Once the latency stage is over, however, the patient is ready to recognize without self-deceptions that he or she is living a sick relationship and is ready for a change on the behavioral level: the relationship must end at all costs.

Phase 3. Implementation or active abstinence

During the latency phase, the patient has analyzed his or her emotional present and experienced it from a new perspective. Now, the addiction is considered as a sort of "obligation", a cage it's hard to go out from, something which leads to the same results through repeated behaviors. Contrary to the first phase, the patient now has a clearer vision of reality: the relationship is sick and needs to be changed, before it's too late. What confirms that a patient is ready to start the implementation phase is the change in choosing the terms to be used: he or she doesn't use terms such as "love", "make love" and prefers similar expressions.

Furthermore, the patient starts to erase the partner's idealized portrait, to see his or her problems and weaknesses, which generally bring the love addiction basis into question. The implementation phase is a moment in which the patient decides to leave the love object. The decision is made in an autonomous and painful way. People who interrupt a love addiction experience a grief and expose themselves to a trauma; so, this phase of the psychotherapy is not painless.

Even though most part of the job has been carried out, the patient has to face a real abstinence syndrome just like in the detoxification from psychoactive substances. Headache, abdominal pains, insomnia, irritability, anxiety are the most frequent symptoms in the first days of active abstinence.

During some phases, the psychic pain is so intense that "relapses" can occur: searching for or meeting the partner diminish the abstinence syndrome and actually make the change process last longer. One of the most serious problems when facing a "detoxification" is that the drug the patient is addicted to "has legs" so it can chase the victim, try to convince him or her and take the control again. I saw a lot of patients during this phase, turning from chaser into chased, struggling to refuse the other.

Another enemy to fight during the active addiction phase is a phenomenon known in drug addictions or in other type of addictions: craving.

Craving is an uncontrollable impulse which attacks the victim through a slight contact with the object of the addiction, which leads to uncontrollable consumption.

In alcohol addictions, the craving phenomenon goes from "just a sip then I'll stop!" to the consumption of liters of alcoholic beverages until the loss of consciousness. In love addiction, for example, craving consists in sending to the partner just a text message to know how he or she is and then finding themselves to make love with or begging him or her for more attention.

The problem with craving is that it is impossible to be repressed. Therefore, the only solution is to avoid any exposure to the addiction object, being aware that there are no ways to manage the addiction and that it has to be stopped.

The active addiction phase is the last critical stage of psychotherapy, since a strong sense of belonging to the pathological relationship still remains. Relapses can occur, the patient can keep deceiving himself or herself and meeting the love object; this can even lead to a therapeutic path interruption. However, if the work has been positive so far, the love addiction circle is now worn-out, deformed, it no longer gives the illusion that everything will come back as before. So, even in cases of relapses or those in which the patients give up on therapy, the change is already started and, even if slowly and painfully, it will keep going on until it won't be completed.

The "active addiction" phase lasts until the patient is aware of his or her efforts, until he or she misses the partner and the old dynamics. During this phase, the patient progressively experiences a sort of "detoxification" at the end of which the patient will realize that he or she has stopped to brood, to feel bad and to depend on the relationship or its idea. The signals of a change are represented by behaviors more than thoughts: there are no more immediate replies to text messages, people and objects which recall the other person are taken away and so on.

Once this fundamental goal is reached, it is possible to start the following phase.

Phase 4. Corrective emotional experience

The period of active abstinence generally entails a concrete and unplanned change in a person's daily life. The "voids" left by the addiction are gradually filled with new interests and activities. The ex-addicted experiences in a different way most of the things and surprisingly feels a growing pleasure and satisfaction in the everyday life. Working is satisfactory again, the meetings with friends are more frequent and stimulating; it is not rare that this subject acquires the ability to take care of himself or herself. In this phase, the therapeutic meetings are surprising, with new stories and comments on unexpected experiences. The patient acquires the ability to emotionally take part in events and to express his or her own feelings through a non-verbal communication rich of shades. It is like talking with a child who is discovering the world, someone who has just woken up from an evil spell, after a very long sleep; someone who is tasting the beauty of what surrounds him or her.

At the same time, the patient almost doesn't talk about the love object which is now a source of sorrow, not of nostalgia. His or her thoughts tend to go back to the past relationship, but contrary to what occurred in the previous phases, he or she doesn't mention the emotional pain and devastation not to get stuck in its debris.

During this phase, there are one or two crucial moments which permit to break the addiction patterns. These events are emotionally intense and characterized by a different self-perception. For this reason, these moments lead to therapeutic consequences which correct the way of thinking that in the past fed the addiction vicious circles. Examples of corrective emotional experiences can be an encounter with a new person the patient feels attracted to; a trip lived in full independence, without any "supporting friend" as such in the past and without the worrying wait for a message or a phone call just like at the times of the love addiction.

Emotive experiences vary according to the subject and are not necessarily extraordinary events. What is "corrective", "therapeutic" is not the fact that it occurs, but the perception of it, a new, free and serene perception.

Now, more than ever, the patient gets closer to realize about the abyss he or she has fallen; now, more than ever, he or she is able to rejoice in being escaped from that abyss. A clear signal which permits us to understand that the patient is at this stage is the fact that he or she starts to surprisingly ask himself or herself: "How was it possible for me to be a slave in a so unhappy relationship? How could I do that?".

Phase 5. Awareness Phase

In this phase, which is generally short, the patient realizes about what happened to him or her and is ready to give convincing answers on why and how he or she fell into a pathological addiction. This phase is more rational than emotional, since the patient has already found an emotional balance; now, the dynamics which caused the problem and the strategies which solved it have to be consciously analyzed.

Sometimes, awareness has a painful impact. The patient can "discover" he or she was just an object or that the partner took advantage of him or her for sex or money. So, this is also the phase of the anger against himself or herself and the other person, the moment when a point of no return is set.

During this therapeutic phase, the patient serenely faces the fundamental traits of his or her own identity, such as the need of belonging to someone, the love desire, the quality of the relationships with parents, relatives and friends. The result is a new analysis of priorities in daily life and in relationships.

The new question made to the therapist is: "How do I know that I won't do the same mistake? How do I know that I won't replace an addiction with another one?". This problem can be solved if the patient decides to have a "healthy addiction" to the person he or she loves. A healthy addiction can be characterized by concepts such as reciprocity, trust, independence, open-mindedness and tendency to make plans. These features are all opposite to the pathological addiction.

Other criteria to distinguish the "healthy" from the "pathological" relationship are:

- the ability to maintain and respect private spaces and manage them without causing control or jealousy reactions
- tolerating the partner's physical absence;
- living the relationship without the fear of a possible end or abandonment.

Phase 6. Consolidation

The consolidation phase is the final one and it aims at supporting the patient in acquiring freedom and stability. Even if faced with the best strategies, a love addiction story leaves in its protagonists consequences which make them doubtful, anxious and, sometimes, extremely suspicious about new love relationships.

Furthermore, the disappearance of symptoms and dysfunctional behaviors (absence of social life, constant focusing on symptoms, constant request for help) which characterized family life and friendships, often unveils the existence – also in these "healthy" relationships – of problems and "mechanisms" which the "recovered addicted" firmly and suddenly refuses after years of condescension. A reaction to a change from the patient's friends or relatives is not always positive. "You're no longer who you used to be" is the accusation which the former patients can hear after gaining independence.

The consolidation sessions help the patient in creating a new way of living in the social context and searching for new challenges. The therapist's role in these last steps is to underline - from time to time - the progress made and push the patient to keep going on his or her own, being confident of the results obtained. The sessions are always less frequent: once per month, once every two months and so on until the last one, when all the progresses are summarized and future scenarios are outlined.

Generally, the consolidation signals are clearly visible and tell the therapist that it is time to end the therapy. Besides the complete symptoms remission and the resumption of the activities the patient stopped doing during the addiction period, at the end of psychotherapy the patient tends to speak about his or her traumatic events at the past tense; he or she recalls them with indifference and without a visible suffering.

On a concrete level, it is not rare that the patient decides to overcome the limits which he or she previously considered as part of his or her own personality. For example, there are patients who decide to go living on their own or to eventually fight their professional dissatisfaction.

The consolidation phase has a variable duration according to the cases; generally, it is between five and eight appointments in one year. In such a long period it is possible to evaluate the "endurance" of the change and help the patient in facing possible threatening events. One of these usually consists in the attempt of the addiction object to start a new relationship with the ex-addicted.

For the patient it can be a critical circumstance: why did he/she refuse him/her and now he/she is coming back? Why is the tormentor so tender now? Why is he/she promising to change and love me eternally?

At this point, the patient has the necessary tools to see how cruel and perverse was the communicative circle he/she was stuck into. I often ask to those who have finished the therapy to write their impressions on the work we made, to evaluate the results and the solidity of their change; I have received very moving and lucid answers. Among the most frequent answers there are a strong sensation of freeing themselves and the real possibility to live a new love with joy.

Eight therapeutic strategies to break the love addiction patterns

Wisdom
is letting what is born grow,
enjoying what is ripe
and forgetting about what is dead.
(Shafique Keshavjee)

In the middle of the 70's, a group of American psychiatrists and psychologists – later known as the Palo Alto School of Psychology (California) – wanted to discuss a dogma which had been untouched until then: the change occurs gradually, requires a long time and several years of psychotherapy. The need to re-analyze this requirement came from the unsatisfactory results of long-term therapies based on the analysis of the past and subconscious, and from new discoveries within fields which seemed to be distant from psychology such as cybernetics, mathematics and physics: according to these discoveries, change is not necessarily slow and gradual, but a short and "revolutionary" process.

The challenge against long-term psychotherapy proposed by the Palo Alto School of Psychology and following generations of short-term psychotherapists has been won after several decades.

Nowadays, there are hundreds of international studies which highlight the effectiveness of the short-term approaches in most of the therapies for psychological disorders (anxiety, panic attacks, phobias, obsession, reactive and non-reactive depression). Then, starting from strategic psychotherapies and "traditional" models, "light" versions of such models have been designed. Even psychoanalysis, the dinosaur of psychotherapies, today is divided in tens of short-term psychoanalysis.

One of the characteristics of the strategic approach to human problems is the use of rules and tasks which the patients have to carry out and respect between the sessions; this seems weird but is effective in solving problems in short periods of time. The therapist has an active role in the change process, stimulates the patient's actions towards new directions, showing to him or her – at first at an experience level and then at the emotional and cognitive ones – the mechanisms the addiction is based on and tries to break them. Strategic brief psychotherapies start from a simple and fundamental assumption: to solve a problem it takes to start from "how does it work?" instead of trying to understand the reason why it exists (Nardone, Watzalawick, 1990). In fact, although the patient is aware of the "deep" origins of a problem (past family dynamics? Childhood traumas?), this rarely is sufficient to make him or her change the unconscious strategies he or she uses every day to complicate his or her relationship. This is true in love addictions, since a person go to therapy with a sophisticated idea of himself or herself and his or her story with a series of "why" this happened to him or her; although the patient's explanations seem to be logical and reasonable, the pathology persists and gets worse. It is clear that the emotional difficulties and their solutions are not based on a linear logic.

So, searching for a rational explanation for the vicious circles of love pains is like trying to fix a broken mirror with nails and hammer: the best intentions lead to a bigger damage. The strategic psychotherapy, therefore, works on the "irrational" aspects which feed the psychic suffering and, instead of fighting, it uses them for a change. In order to do it, the therapist opts for a hypnotic communication, rich of anecdotes, analogies and metaphors to talk to the patient's "irrational mind", the one which has the control of his or her life during the love addiction period. Then, the patient is involved in an active and concrete change process through specific rules and tasks, aiming at breaking the solid pattern of the pathology. The choice of a therapeutic strategy aims at interrupting the series of actions, emotions and behaviors which feeds the dysfunctional relationship; obviously there isn't an effective strategy for all cases. Each person follows a personalized path, created according his or her specific values, expectations and attitudes.

For this reason, the eight strategies I describe in this chapter have an illustrative purpose and represent only a small sample of the endless possibilities the therapist can choose – according to the type of patient – to come to a long-lasting change in a small number of sessions.

In more than fifty years of history, the strategic approach to human problems has reached a high level of development which now allows us to prove the effectiveness of some strategies on specific problems. For example, we have now a wide literature on anxiety and panic attacks, depressions and food disorder treatments. The methods showed in this volume are inspired by other successful ones on specific pathologies; they are the result of a direct application on tens of cases. From this perspective, they represent a new and original contribution – even if not definitive – to the treatment of love addictions. The methods described as follows can surely inspire the therapists who want to act as soon as possible on this kind of problems; for laymen, it can be a cause for reflection on themselves and how to start a change in their way of living the dysfunctional love relationship, whether necessary.

The silence task

"For the therapy to be immediately effective it is important that you carry out a task during this week.

From now until the next session you mustn't speak to other people about your relationship and your feelings.

Stay silent and, if you fail, which I believe you'll do, remember that the more you speak, the more you make the situation worse"-

To Pascal, "Silence is more valuable to love than words" but, usually men and women trapped in a love addiction act in an opposite way. A dysfunctional attempt to solve a problem in an unhappy relationship is, in fact, to talk with relatives, friends or acquaintances about it, searching for an advice on how to get out of the crisis. More often, love addicted people put their efforts in a real propaganda of their story with the unconscious request for support because of the injustice they feel to be victims of.

The tendency to tell about their own feelings in details, in fact, seems to alleviate anguish and loneliness, while the advices received from other people give the illusion of control on a feeling. Unfortunately, the relief after sharing feelings with other people doesn't last long and, when it disappears, the addicted person starts to unburden himself or herself to other people over again.

The frequency this happens with causes two effects. Friends and acquaintances start to dissociate themselves from the patient or start a fight together with the patient against love pains, giving useless suggestions – in the best case – which are often counterproductive.

If the level of the addiction reaches the highest level, the addicted person - more or less openly - refuses any opinion different than his or hers and reacts aggressively towards those who suggest to interrupt the relationship with the love object. So, a series of "secondary addictions" appears within the addicted person's social context; these addictions come from a compulsive communication and an unhealthy attachment to one or more friends or relatives who were asked to help him or her.

His or her friends, at a certain moment, may think their support is effective but then they discover it is not.

Sometimes they see the addicted subject angry, determined to interrupt the relationship and regain control of his or her own life; within a few days, they'll see him or her back on square one, delirious and dreamy for a love he or she believes in again.

The people who try to help the addicted person become a sort of palliative until they unconsciously feed the addiction. Also when the addiction relationship ends, the complicity of parents and friends while listening and supporting the "victim" feeds the psychological blackout which sustains the addiction.

It is known that the more we talk about something, the more it becomes real, even if this indisputable fact clashes with the socially shared belief that unburdening ourselves is good. Real "social groups" start to gather around the love addicted, a sort of powerless talking audience which, almost every day, watches the inevitable fall of the protagonist of an authentic drama. Indirectly, the audience ends up pushing him or her to go on, to keep fighting towards self-destruction. The advisers chosen by the love addicted surely act with noble intentions, but then they become one of the causes of the problem. From this perspective, "talking" about the problem represents one of the main mechanisms which lead to the problem persistence.

Therefore, we have to understand that the "silence task" is a fundamental therapeutic strategy which can lead to great results in treating the love addiction. This task works directly on the communicative system which strengthens the addiction, since the patient's sudden silence interrupts the vicious circle which feeds itself on the things he or she has told in confidence.

The same method is a classic of the strategic brief therapy for anxiety disorders and panic attacks, a field in which it has led to great results according to international studies on wide clinical samples (Nardone, 1993, Nardone, Watzlawick, 2005).

The anxious patient constantly asks for help and receives the indirect message "I help you because you're not able to do it", which confirms a self-perception of inadequacy which feeds the symptom; in the same way, the love addicted gets stuck in a social system which is supposed to help him or her, but conveys implicit belittling messages and makes the addiction grow.

A lot of patients reluctantly accept the silence task, others consider it as an immediate possibility to change. But in both cases, this task leads to useful effects to break a first circuit of love addiction.

Those who follow this prescription generally show a symptoms reduction: the obsession diminishes while the perception of controlling the problem grows. Those who don't carry out the "silence task" will be able to understand and feel how deep the addiction is and, above all, will realize that the more they relies on their confidants, the worse it will be.

This discovery pushes the addicted person to put more efforts during psychotherapy and regain, week after week, control on his or her impulsiveness.

A further benefit is an easier direct problem analysis with no needs for thoughts, emotions and behaviors to be filtered by other people's opinions. During the therapy, this allows to talk about the past experiences within the short time of a session, gradually separating the patient from the constant thought of the relationship he or she is addicted to.

The addiction "diary"

"To intervene on your obsession, we need to collect as more data as possible, so it is important that you don't do anything different than before the therapy started, from now until the next session.

Try not to change; the more you'll feel addicted, the better it will be for us.

Therefore, this week write in a diary all your obsessions the same time they appear: as soon as you feel they're coming, describe them in details with date, time, people you were with, symptoms, emotions and thoughts..."

The diary method is common in different therapeutic approaches. In the love addiction treatment, this prescription goes beyond the accurate and detailed description of anxious and depressive events lived by the patient, even if this is the motivation the task is introduced with. Actually, on a strategic level, this method allows to convey more therapeutic messages:

1. *"go slow"*: when underlining that the patient doesn't have to change immediately, the therapist alleviates the urgency sense and the impulsiveness;

2. *"symptoms are useful"*: by requesting to start a sort a diagnostic phase, the therapist indirectly suggests a new and valuable concept on the pathology: the symptoms appearance is useful to solve the problem. This new concept of suffering allows the patient to put symptoms and negative events within the new frame of a possible change.

3. *"move the attention"*: writing in a diary at the very moment of the problem appearance entails the immediate benefit of moving the attention from the symptoms to the act of writing. Generally, after one or two weeks, this task leads to a "magical" suffering decrease while, at the same time, increases the awareness of the patient's addiction patterns.

Although it seems simple, the addiction "diary" method is effective and flexible, since it can be changed according to the type of problem. For example, when dealing with a pathological jealousy and its relative behaviors of control and surveillance, the patient is asked to choose "Notebook of the little detective" as the diary title; he or she is also asked to describe the "investigations" in details and their influence on his or her mood. Also in this method, the psychological impact of the diary is based on a therapeutic trick. First of all, it leads to a new indirect definition of the obsessive control strategies within a "playful" frame and, at the same time, it leads the patient to think that his or her own behaviors are childish and harmful. Acting as the "little detective" causes an intense loathing towards pathological obsession and the jealousy feeling; it also leads, in a short period of time, to the symptoms disappearance.

The "desperate letters"

"Get the most beautiful writing paper and envelopes with the color you like the most, choose everything accurately.

When you'll feel the biggest pain, go in front of the mirror and get prepared to go out: you will have to look sad, depressed, wrecked, so don't wear bright colors and don't put your makeup on.

Just like an actress in a romantic movie, take paper, envelopes and your favorite pen and go to the most scenic place of the city, for example a café in the city centre or an elegant square.

Once there, sit down and write the most intense and saddest love letter. It has to start with "Dear X, my hopeless love…"

The patients generally are astonished by this task. The therapist asks them to express in public their anguish by writing letters. The implicit logic is one of the cornerstones of short-term strategic psychotherapies: the symptom prescription. Basically, the patient is indirectly asked to take possession of the symptom instead of suffering from it: this leads to surprising results. If the patient carries out the task, he or she will initially feel bad, but not more than usual; but when writing the following desperate letters, the patient will experience a gradual desensitization towards the problem and the entire love relationship. The abandonment and frustration feelings, which are voluntarily repeated, gradually lose their meaning and the patient starts to distance himself or herself from them.

Furthermore, the idea of the outside scenic background forces the patient not to stay locked inside his or her house suffering and, at the same time, makes the symptoms turn into something ridiculous; this radically changes the perspective on the impossible return to the object of the love obsession. By carrying out this task, the patient learns how to fight the suffering, to move from a passive attitude to an active one, aware of the need to get rid of the problem as soon as possible.

In case the patient, during the week after the therapeutic prescription refuses to write the letters, the prescription is successful anyway, since it proves that he or she has the control of the problem and can stop the suffering, if he or she wants. The patient, not only won't carry out the task but, thanks to the suggestive power of the request, he or she will avoid the situations which feed the problem, such as text messages sending, useless pursuits or the compulsive request for help.

The prescription of the "desperate letters", in a context of love addiction, leads to a paradox: whether the patient refuses or accepts to carry it out, the symptoms slowly disappear, while the awareness of being in an absurd relationship grows. So, the patient is also aware that the problem can be solved with a radical change in the way of facing it.

If the patient doesn't write his "despaired letters", he or she realizes to have unexpected resources: he or she goes to the cinema, to the gym, goes back to work, accepts invitations which in the past he or she would have refused.

These are behaviors which lead to a concrete change and the patient is always less focused on the addiction and the dysfunctional relationship.

The metaphor

With metaphors it is possible to communicate extremely significant and complex messages to the patient, bypassing his or her resistance. Metaphors use expressions and images which seem to be distant from the patient, expressed in a language which is open to more interpretations and meanings.

The evocative contents of anecdotes, fairy tales and other stories reach more easily the patient's right hemisphere (which is the area of emotions and creativity); they stimulate creativity and emotions, "paralyzing" the left hemisphere, the area of the logical thought, which often prevents us to observe ourselves, the outside world and the other people differently from our usual way (Secci, 2005, page 74).

When treating love addictions, the use of metaphors is quite necessary since, although the patient recognizes his or her actions as rationally inadequate and the absurdity of the relationship, he or she is not able to avoid the problem. In fact, the addiction always involves emotions and it is only based on psycho-logical reasons. By telling metaphorical anecdotes, the therapist can directly stimulate the emotional nucleus which supports the addiction more than with any other types of rational tools.

Metaphors in psychotherapy, to be successful must be personalized, so to be specific and evocative for the patient. These are some examples:

"One day, a little boy, alone in the street, felt attracted by the shining lights of a Casino.

He only had three coins in his pockets and he didn't want to waste them gambling, but the building doors seemed so big and welcoming that he got in but not to play, just to have a look.

Once there, he got struck by slot-machines.

They were beautiful and the people seated in front of them looked hypnotized.

"What if I only use a coin?", the little boy thought. A moment later, he started playing. Nothing happened.

"I've lost one coin, but I still can win. I shouldn't, but I can do it". Again, nothing happened.

"I've already lost two coins, I shouldn't... but I'll spend the last one".
The slot-machine, with its light and triumphant music spit out only five coins.
"What a stroke of luck!", the little boy cried out.
So he played again... and lost all his money".

Giorgio, trapped in a thirteen-year-old marriage, listened to this metaphor just before the end of the session. The first months of his relationship with Alessandra were good "but not awesome", he said. Soon after the wedding, almost unilaterally, and after a constant pressure by Alessandra and her family, the relationship quickly got worse. But despite of his attempts to improve the relationship, he realized he was dealing with a depressed woman, addicted to her parents who also made all the decisions on the marriage.

The sexual harmony, which initially was good, soon become a rare and awkward reproductive ritual, since Alessandra, bored and passive, wanted a son to make the marriage complete.

More than any other psycho-dynamic and rational explanations, the story helped Giorgio in realizing how his relationship was working: betting always more on a frustrating and endless game, trying in vain to adapt himself to a relationship started for fear of being lonely, with the illusion to quickly grow so to escape from a broken home and the doubts on his sexual identity which used to oppress him as an adolescent.

Monica - trapped in a destructive relationship with Guido from more than three years - went to therapy totally worn-out, after the umpteenth pseudo-separation. The metaphor use caused an overwhelming effect. Like in the past, Guido humiliated Monica in public and, in the same evening, once they were alone, he punished her with the cruel refrain "I can't love someone like you", followed by long and humiliating list of lacks and flaws, both physical and emotional. She was devastated. Then, she had two terrible weeks, which started with her self-punitive behaviors: she stopped eating, cried every day and started to suffer from insomnia and panic attacks. When she started the therapy, though, she also realized about the flaws of the relationship and decided to free herself from Guido, who was turning from Prince Charming into a sadistic jailer. Monica's recovery was very fast: she started eating regularly, focusing on her work and living the social life Guido has never allowed her to live. Just before he – as usually occurs in love addictions – reappeared again, I told Monica this story:

"A woman found a snake in her garden. It was very small and looked like it was fragile and lonely. She decided to take care of it. She did. She gave it food and something to drink and it seemed that the snake was thankful. They spent a lot of years together until the snake grew up and it was no longer possible to keep it in a snake tank, so the woman let it move around the house free. When the animal got ill again, she took it to the veterinary who cured it.

One morning, the woman woke up and saw the snake lying on the bed beside her, staring at her, still and rigid as a stick. After the initial fear, she started to worry because it kept remaining still and, since it didn't give sign of life, she desperately called the veterinary. "Come now, I've found the snake totally rigid on my bed! Is it dead!? Help me!"

The veterinary suddenly answered: "I'm coming, but get away immediately from your house. The snake is taking your measurements."

Monica reacted with disgust and said she didn't understand the reason why I had used this metaphor, considering that Guido disappeared for good, since he didn't want to stay with her. Even though she decided to interrupt the relationship, Monica was still trapped in the lack of self-esteem she got used to at the time of the relationship. However, when he – as he used to do – called her on the phone again, Monica, for the first time left the phone on the bedside table and finally felt to be free.

The worst conditions

"What should you do to make this negative situation even worse? Think about it every day and list the things that come to your mind, but don't put them into practice".

This question, called "worst fantasy", is used in strategic psychotherapy to solve several types of problems (anxiety, panic attacks, depressions and food disorders) (Nardone, 1993, 1999); it is also successful with love addiction. Pushing a patient to deeply think about how he or she could make the situation worse allows him or her to discover - day after day – that behaviors, emotions and thoughts which could cause more pain are those he or she has always put into practice. At least at the initial stage, they were useful to temporarily solve the problem. Therefore, searching for solutions to an intentional worsening leads to two possible goals: it makes the patient realize about his or her responsibilities in maintaining the dysfunctional relationship alive and also makes the identified negative behaviors disappear.

For example, while thinking of the question, Lucia finally admitted that long and frustrating nights spent sending text messages made frustration and suffering grow, since they forced her to wait for cold replies such as "Good night" or "Fine, thank you". So, she stopped sending text messages to him for an entire week and noticed a mood improvement.

It can happen that some answers to "which is the worst possible situation?" are: "Things will get worse if he/she will tell me he or she doesn't want to see me again" or "Things will get worse if he/she sees another man/woman". Also in this case the prescription is useful since it permits to deal with a fundamental aspect in love addictions, which is the fear of being refused and the tendency to think about a possible acceptance which is, basically, illusory. Processing the fear to be refused and admitting that it is more painful to keep living a unilateral relationship than facing the suffering due to disappointed expectations can become clear therapeutic goals; they can also make the patient's behaviors and perception more functional.   .

A Men's report card

"From now to the next session, please write a list of physical and emotional qualities, for example, face, body, pleasantness, openness to relationships etcetera and also, according to these qualities, fill in a report card for each man you meet.

Please, give a mark from 0 to 10, as if we were at school.

You will have to evaluate at least 4 people and, please, be objective!"

This prescription aims at moving the patient's focus towards the outside world and helping him/her in recognizing the isolation and refusal patterns he/she is trapped into after a constant attention to the dysfunctional relationship. This is an example of a prescription for a female heterosexual patient, but it can be adapted, if necessary, to male patients.

Generally, this task is accepted with surprise and can lead to several effects, all useful for the change process. Some people carry out the task and accurately analyze the chosen subjects, highlighting their flaws. In conclusion, all the subjects are not good. This starts a discussion on the idealization of the addiction object and the inflexibility the patient approaches the outside world with; this makes the patient think about the possibility of a new relationship.

In other cases, the patient comes to the next session with "positive" report cards: thanks to this task, he or she notices interesting subjects for possible relationships and starts to think that the escape plan is not so hard to be carried out.

Whatever the contents of these report cards are, this task requests to assign the patient the active role of "judge", to help him or her in developing an aware opinion on the way he or she approaches the relationship with.

When love addiction develops in an asymmetrical couple - where a partner is prevailing - the request to "give marks" can be referred to the prevailing partner's behavior. Also in this way, the "report cards" method indirectly changes the perception of passivity and inflexibility which characterizes the patient's way to live the relationship; it gives the idea of "power" on the relationship.

It also highlights the abyss between what the patient wants from the partner and what the partner actually does, between what the partner is expected to be and what he or she actually is.

The "love return" prediction

"As soon as you will try to go away, he will let you go; he will seem not to care about it.

He knows he has the control.

Then, when you will be better, as it happens always more frequently, and you'll show him you can live without his anger, he will come back.

You'll see. He will try to get in touch with you, trying to recapture you with messages full of insults or a bunch of roses. Maybe, by begging.

He'll do it. Then, how will you act?"

The prediction of the "love return" aims at supporting and strengthening the changes reached with the therapy, when the relationship cannot be recovered, since it's based on the victim-tormentor pattern.

While symptoms and disorientation showed by the patient slowly reduce, the contacts with the partner proportionately diminish. This happens because the therapeutic conversations indirectly show how "toxic" the interactions with the love object are; these interactions are always the same, they lead to abandonment. When the patient realizes about the pathological dynamics, he or she autonomously tries to reduce or eliminate his or her involvement in the relationship, with suffering and a sense of failure. For this reason, the therapist predicts the "love return" on two levels: on one hand, the therapist indirectly comforts the inner "part" of the patient which is still addicted; on the other hand, he or she tells to the strong "part" of the patient that the partner is an active member of the relational catastrophe and has the pathological need for someone to be addicted to him or her. These two levels allow the patient to go on with the therapy with the useful thought that "maybe the relationship is not over yet"; meanwhile, he or she comes to the idea that a return would be the confirmation of the pathological relationship he or she wants to get rid of. When the partner returns, the patient is well-prepared, less addicted and capable to avoid the relationship traps thanks to the prediction. If, the "return" doesn't occur, the prediction allows the patient to have the time to get out of the addiction and, therefore, to suffer less for the partner loss.

The Hollywood movie

One of the main features of the love addiction is the idealization of partner and relationship.

At the peak of the problem, the addicted person constantly thinks about his or her partner and the relationship, which is considered as a lost Eden. Without openly facing this specific aspect - which would make the patient feel misunderstood and damage the therapeutic alliance - the therapist can opt for a paradoxical prescription:

"I ask you to find 21 minutes every day. It is important for you to have a bit of space for your thoughts with the exercise I'm going to ask you to do.

Every day, for 21 minutes, you will have to sit on a comfortable chair in a silent room, where nobody can interrupt your activity and think in the most intense way about the beauty of your lost Paradise.

Try to think about the most beautiful faces of history and the best ones: imagine the most vivid colors, choose a soundtrack and all the necessary features to transform it into a great Hollywood movie.

At the end of the time, you will close your eyes, imagining a completely dark screen, as if you were at the cinema at the end of an awesome movie".

The technique of the Hollywood movie is a sort of "symptom prescription": the patient is asked to do, in a magnified way and for a limited period of time, what he or she spontaneously and usually does. Furthermore, the request to add some fantastic and grandiose features in an idealized scenario makes the exercise more effective. Very often, during the following session, the patient shows an improvement, since the 21 minutes of thinking repeated every day become so unbearable that in the rest of the following days they significantly reduce. By "creating" the symptom, the patient experiences a new sense of control on the problem, together with an increasing awareness of the fact that, without the fantastic inventions added during these 21 minutes, the relationship is anything but a romantic novel.

Obviously, it is not possible to adapt the task to specific cases and, during the therapy period, to change the duration according to the patient's response.

Ruggero, a 35 year-old man, obsessed by his relationship with Giulia, was surprised when he was given the prescription. "This will make me feel as bad as ever", he said. He had been living locked in an atrocious grief, recalling the beautiful moments with his ex - which were rare pauses in a sort of cruel game – as if they were the most representative ones. This caused insomnia and distracted him from work and social life. He still considered dating other women as "cheating on" Giulia. At the next session, he said he couldn't carry out the Hollywood movie prescription because just thinking of locking himself inside a room frightened him. But he said that the thoughts were diminishing and he felt better. This means that the task works even if not carried out, since it encourages the patient to acquire control and awareness of the thoughts which feed the addiction, to manage them without suffering.

Stories

Thousands of stories and comments have been posted on the blog or sent to my e-mail address. A lot of people felt the need to talk about their painful love relationship, to ask questions about the perverse narcissist's "nature". Often, the blog users have talked to each other in the comments section: they have exchanged advices, encouraging each other to overcome a dark period of their life. Within the blog, a small "self-help group" has indirectly influenced the contents posted during the last years.

Sometimes, the quantity of requests for help from the Internet was so high that I preferred writing a post in the blog to answer them.

This book partially fulfills the need to answer to a lot of messages received from women and men who have realized to be "victims" of a love addiction with a pathological narcissist or at least to be trapped in "impossible relationships" described in the blog. I have decided to publish some of the stories posted on the blog from the website www.enricomariasecci.blog.tiscali.it to give voice to those who wrote to me, believing that the stories published in this chapter can contribute to make tolerance, acceptance and solutions for non-love relationships more profound, shared and human.

Kiaretta

I feel the need to talk with someone who can understand me. I start by saying that I'm in a relationship from three years with a perverse narcissist, I'm sure of it, but I'm his lover and, besides suffering for the way he is, I obviously suffer for his "being busy", but this is another matter. I don't want to tell all the details also because I saw that the plot is always the same. I'm aware of who he is, but also of who I am for starting a relationship like this. I read a lot of stories and this should help me.

But, do you know what keeps me stuck in this situation? The thought that maybe he acts like this only with me, while with his wife he is a different person; that he escapes and returns only with me; that he loves to punish only me (since when we argue he punishes me by disappearing and not answering to my desperate messages in which I beg him to talk with him etc.); that he is ambiguous only with me to make me doubt about him and so on. Is it possible that I'm so silly to imagine his wife falling asleep with a smile on her face? To imagine her proud and happy to have this man beside her? I must say first that he has always cheated on her, also when they got married, he had an affair for two years which kept going on even after the wedding... he says he has married her because she is calm, she doesn't bother him... while I always ask for explanations on anything; he considers me as a pain in the a**!!

When we meet and stay together for an entire day, he finds an excuse and she doesn't ask for explanations. Anyway, I've decided we're done and I'll ask help to a therapist even if I still can't think the separation is the solution. (...)

Matteo

(...) Yesterday she woke me up in the middle of the night... don't leave me alone, please... and then she said Because you are an idiot with a big problem... I have a problem and tomorrow I'm going to search for someone who can help me, but your problem is bigger than mine... I thought... I want to smile again, to feel the sun inside me, which is exactly what I always give to everybody, a beautiful smile... But I have to say that I've grown up a lot, I feel as I've changed... hope to get out of it as soon as possible... totally... thanks for creating this website.

Alessandra

Thank you Doctor for all the articles you wrote on love addiction and the descriptions of what happens in reality. I have been victim of a narcissist, a parasite who has driven anyone away. He has used me both at a professional and personal level. I used to do anything for him, to make his life simpler. He alternated sweet moments, when he showered me with compliments, with moments in which he said that I was nothing, mentally ill, a mad person since I started reacting to his manipulations. I have humiliated myself in front of other people, really looking like as a mad person; he was always perfect in front of the other people and I was the one who attacked him. I saw his manipulations and his attempts of seducing other women and I could not do anything because he used to say "You're paranoid!!". I had to leave my job, which I adored. I have isolated myself from my family and friends. He told me that, by leaving him I would have remained alone, that I was alone without him, or when I tried to get away from him, he said that he needed me. He has always convinced me. He has destroyed me as a woman and a professional. I feel that I haven't got out yet. Sometimes, I would like to call him, send him a text message, I'm scared that he might forget about me. But then I recall everything he has done, the pain he caused me and tell myself I deserve more... I can say that in a situation like mine, a big help is needed. I've been going to therapy for a year and a half and only after one year I managed to get away from him. I know that there is still much to do. Now, I'm working on it. I hope one day to tell myself "Now I'm finally happy".

Abracadabra

(...) My relationship has lasted 2 years and it was devastating, it is for everybody. It's important to say that I used to read on the Internet too... I must have read all blogs and articles on the borderline disorder, even thesis... I knew everything on this type of disorder... but I understood nothing... or I couldn't or I didn't want to understand. One day, after the umpteenth argue... I actually saw who he really was... these people are not evil and horrible as they seem... they are people with significant disorders which do not allow them to live happily, so they ruin their own and other people's life... they don't do it because we are not enough for them... they would do it with anyone... on the contrary, the more we are important for them, the worse is for them... the more they can't be in a relationship with us... I have suffered a lot... but I don't blame him... and also I don't blame myself because I think it could happen to everybody... I've just realized and experienced that having a relationship with him is impossible because I can't manage it... He can't have an intimate relationship with me or any other woman he really likes... what a pity! I like him... but I really can't do anything... It seems strange... to us... to me it seemed absurd... because I'm not like this... but it takes to enter in these people's head and you will get that they are like this! I think this is the conclusion we all have to come and understand, then we have to face the problem that pushed us in this addiction. It took me 8 months of therapy but it was worth it... now I'm really good and I can live my life!

Dalia

(...) I think I'm one of the few people who have lived with a perverse narcissist for ten years. He was my colleague... three months ago I left him and now I live on my own with my kids (one of my three is also his son)... I think I've passed all the real perverse narcissist phases in these years... until last year I had been thinking about the positive things I'd done with him together with the negative aspects (he's affectless, mean with me and my son, moods swings from one hour to another, he was in constant touch with his ex and other women... blackmails for money etc.)

I keep working on it with him, but I've decided that the only communication we can have is because of our son, he has publicly offended me on facebook... but I keep going, with my head held high, trying not to turn back... it could be dangerous... I still don't know if I'm out of it... (...)

Ale

(...) I had a relationship of this type which has destroyed me little by little until I had to go to a psychiatrist and then to therapy. When the first abandonment happened I still was strong enough to react. I thought he has left me for good and I recovered quite well but then he came back and we started over again until he found another woman and left me for the second time. Every time I got weaker and weaker. I used to have self-esteem, at least I thought I had it, but then abandonment after abandonment I became addicted to his mood, terrorized by that horrible sensation. He changed suddenly, maybe he didn't accept something about me, such as my freedom. He has left me 5 times before the summer holidays when I told him I was planning to go on a trip because he didn't want to stay with me because of his family (separated with kids). I've never felt a so intense suffering like that. My sense of inadequacy has reached unimaginable levels and I have lived with a sense of guilt. He left me so that I could never get what I did wrong. (...)

Gabriella

(...) Although I had already seen how my narcissist could be mean, I thought: this time he's really changed! But after 3 weeks we were living together, he furiously came home and without a reason packed his bags and went away without an explanation... it was the biggest pain I had ever felt until that moment and, unfortunately other more devastating have followed... I almost committed suicide twice and even thinking of my daughter couldn't help me to go on... every time I did something to go away from him, he came back on a white horse and a sword promising eternal love and total devotion; he made all my certainties weaker; I'm a single mother with a job that is more profitable than his one, totally independent, I've let this sheep disguised as a man humiliate me, hate me, underestimate and offend me physically and mentally; I feel used like a container, like a sexual object... the only thing I couldn't stand was betrayal, so I've put all my efforts in searching for evidences 'til I have found them; hearing from the other woman about the date and the way they've met, humiliated me the most and caused the biggest void inside me but it also pushed me to decide it was over with that evil being who sucked my love and light because he was not able to give love or shine of his own light... only a week has passed, I hate him so much and I realize I love the image he showed me; actually, that awesome and special man who thrills me with a glance doesn't exist, his only goal is to keep being violent... I think he will come back with more powerful weapons, but I will be stronger, I have to be free... I have to start living again...

Silvana

(...) After less than 2 months I fell with my face on the ground from a high floor. His bad habits, his egoism, his indifference and his subtle but cutting irony were slowly appearing again. His criticism and lack of participation in taking care of our house reappeared.

Now I'm at square one and terribly sad. He has dull eyes, an angry gaze.

If he goes out with his friends and I ask him to come back home early, he does it very late. The day after, seeing my disappointment, he apologizes and promises to not do it again. But it does it again. If I go out and I don't come back home at the time he decides, it's war. Spiteful tricks, insults, total lack of responsibility, even towards our kids.

Basically, he is punishing me.

I would like to go No Contact, but would it work?

I would like to leave him, by I'm not so brave... I'm afraid to be wrong, of not deserving love... therefore I withdraw into myself, crying and hoping... that sooner or later he could open his heart to me... because I can't believe he is so empty and insensitive (...) I think of my future and see loneliness with him, I feel like a widow. (...)

Stefano

(...) She knew when to call me back or she waited for me to search for her desperately. She was so afraid I could leave her that when I wasn't happy she got terrorized. She used sex as a prize or a punishment; she didn't tolerate my needs, my feelings, anything.

I used to correct my voice tone when saying something. Typical phrase: you didn't have to tell it that way, but this way. You have disappointed me. I knew that something was going wrong but I wasn't able to leave her. Eventually, I turned into a zombie... I started to somatize. Stress, acute insomnia, rash, depression, nightmares, problems at work, anxiety, uncontrolled jealousy, love addiction was gone sky-high... but she started to be afraid I was about to leave her. My self-protection instinct was emerging and one day, without any warning, she asked me for some time to reflect on us; I refused and she said: "I'm leaving you, I don't love you anymore." (...)

Claudia

(...) He projected on me all his betrayals, he controlled me constantly. I couldn't have a male friend because for him it was a tragedy, but he couldn't stop flirting with every girl he saw, even with girls with the same age of his daughter. He went to bed with all the women who could be useful for his professional life. In Italy or abroad, from musicians to prostitutes, from little girls to transsexuals. I neglected my job, my daughters, my house and a very sweet partner for him. He repaid me with constant humiliations and further shameful lies to cover his attraction for transsexuals. 7 months ago I said goodbye to him, not caring about his depressive crisis and hypothetical disorders. I thank a higher power for having the strength to leave him without getting a serious disease, for protecting my daughters and meeting a wonderful man. This terrible story made me appreciate the value of a man's honest hug, devotion and daily loyalty. I love my husband more than ever, thanks to the MONSTER WHICH SHOWED ME WHAT A MAN IS NOT LIKE.

Annamaria

(...) My narcissist, at the beginning, had an overwhelming enthusiasm, even though I didn't fall in love with him for this reason. However, he soon became dark, cold, a ghost. He was more and more indifferent and fickle, until the refusal, as you call it. He started to postpone our dates and keep saying that we were "in a relationship"! Now that I'm no longer in love with him and his indifference doesn't hurt me, I think that a person like this has some issues. In his head and life. It was good that he is far away now! I feel so lucky! I'm happy now and if I was with him, I think I wouldn't be!

Lili

Thanks to all of you and your thoughts and tormented words. I also identify with this psychological trap and when reading your stories I try to understand, but above all, I don't feel alone. Suffering, illusion, lack of self-esteem, the need to love and being loved, loneliness, psychological fragility have led me to live a sick, destructive and addiction-based relationship.

I want to get out of this psychological prison but it's hard because I felt empty and weak, lost and confused, filled with anxiety and guilt, frightened, sad and at the mercy of emotions, daydreams and despair. I said IT'S ENOUGH, but I told it to myself, I started going to therapy because I want to feel FREE and HAPPY and I won't let anyone to destroy me psychologically.

Little Red Riding Hood in psychotherapy

Little Red Riding Hood is still today one of the most famous fairy tale and it boasts hundreds of reinterpretations: illustrated books, cartoons, audio books and movies.

The original fairy tale, which perhaps is French, dates back to the 14th century and kept acquiring new shades even after its first printed edition of 1697, written by the Parisian story-teller Charles Perrault.

A few people know that the Perrault's fairy tale ending is tragic: the wolf devours Little Red's grandmother and then tears the little girl - who was lying beside it naked - to pieces; but the most famous version is the Grimm brothers' one – from 1857 – in which they change the story ending: a brave woodcutter, finally, rips the wolf's belly open and rescues the little girl and her grandmother from an agonizing death.

Little Red Riding Hood in psychotherapy

We all owe the fascination and the most profound meaning of this fairy tale to psychoanalysis and psychotherapy. Distinguished analysts and therapists have dealt with the clear metaphorical value of Little Red Riding Hood, pushed by the need to unveil the symbols and relational dynamics contained in this fairy tale which has conserved its evocative and suggestive power.

The psychoanalyst Bruno Bettelheim, the author of "The uses of enchantment. The meaning and importance of fairy tales" (1976), carried out a passionate study on Little Red Riding Hood from a profound psychological point of view and proposed an accurate interpretation of its hidden meanings.

The result was the description of an adolescent who, pushed by the emerging needs of her puberty, unconsciously lets herself be devoured by the apparently kind beast.

According to Bettelheim, the wolf is not only "the seducer male": it is also the symbol of "all our existing sensual and antisocial representations" and, as such, it constitutes an irresistible presence for its victim.

Eric Berne (1972) desecrated Little Red by saying that, all things considered, the wolf also has been a victim of a dangerous relational game started by a little girl's ambiguity.

According the founder of the transactional analysis, Little Red is only partially innocent, while the different family-related and emotional disorders which push her to venture into the wood - disobeying her mother - make her the predator's accomplice. In fact, we are dealing with a little girl who intentionally ventures into the wood and talks with the wolf, in an affable and even seductive way, to the point of showing the way to get to her grandmother's house. According to Berne, if Little Red really was, as it seems, detrimental to herself and the other people "... the wolf shouldn't wander alone in the woods!".

Three questions on the love disease

Bettelheim and Berne have described two opposite interpretations of Little Red Riding Hood.

The little girl - more "victim" of her own inner dynamics rather than the wolf - recounted by the first, and the "accomplice" of a self-destructive game unmasked by the second maybe are the two opposite faces of a theoretical continuum which other psychologists have dealt with, trying to answer impossible questions such as: which is the psychological nature of the mortal relationship between the wolf and the little girl? Who is the seducer and who is seduced? Who really is the victim and who is the oppressor?

The same questions arise in all love relationships which turns into desperate - and sometimes fatal - escalations of physical and moral violence; a series of reconciliations, conflicts, threatens, perditions and depressions we call love addiction.

Some women, like in Little Red Riding Wood, have beside them a werewolf who behaves sometimes kindly and sometimes angrily.

There are other women who, being used to their wolf behaviors, lose self-respect and sacrifice everything for him.

Generalizing is impossible, because the love disease can dig into a person's subjectivity to the point of replacing it; each person is unique, as well as it can seem to be for his or her own self-destruction caused by a wolf.

But, besides every single story, all love relationships have in common a specific plot... the Little Red Riding Hood's one.

Inside the metaphor

Little Red Riding Hood keeps enchanting kids and adults and, at the same time, is a study object for love addictions, since it is a metaphor which shows the universal features of pathological love: the little girl, the wolf, the woods.

In my job as a therapist, these features represent the love addicted, her narcissist partner and their relationship.

A relationship which has always been dark and empty, disturbing and fascinating, filled with its protagonists' expectations typical in fairy tales.

In this fairy tale, like in reality, the characters interact in a thick wood, where they give rise to a paradoxical conversation, which is almost dreamlike. The little girl talks with the beast instead of screaming for help or escaping, the animal doesn't bite as it is supposed to do but it observes, asks, as if it was more interested in the seduction which leads to the capture than in the capture itself.

This fairy tale seems to unveil a disturbing feature of reality: the most tempting victims are affable and love their cannibal.

The most important part of this story is the wood.

The wood is the only place where the two characters really meet in all versions and it represents the only moment in which the relationship precedes the abuse and the massacre. Also in the metaphor, the perverse element between the little girl and the wolf is the psychological environment, the destructive relationship represented by the dark wood. The ambiguous communication between the wolf and the little girl is the place in which the premises for a tragic ending come true.

As a therapist, love addiction and the "love disease" came to me through my patients' stories which then turned in requests for help. Anxiety, panic attacks, somatoform disorders (headache, amenorrhea, gastrointestinal dysfunctions etc.), paranoia, hypochondria, depression, obsessions are the loud cry which come from armies of Little Reds in psychotherapy.

In love pains, the symptoms are sort of gags for the desperate people who cry in the wood; these symptoms impede them from seeing themselves as consenting victims, from recognizing the tormentor and getting out of a sick relationship. It is never easy to help who lives a moral violence in going against the wood (the relationship); it is more difficult to understand that his or her pain comes from his or her partner, the wolf, or more precisely, the firm and dark interaction they are forcing themselves to face.

In conclusion, the werewolf is not the partner, but the relationship.

Paola Serino's photographic project

The little girl, the wolf and the wood, also in Paola Serino's photographic project, are the key features of the love disease. Each picture portrays the girl and the wolf in a wood with a freezing atmosphere, hibernated in this relationship which threatens their beauty, the madness of their incompatible distances; they form an impossible separation.

Paola Serino doesn't observe, she shows. She doesn't photograph, she recounts. She recounts of girls and wolves.

But, above all, she talks about resinous woods and emotional labyrinths which lock up all the people who venture into it.

Just like the fairy tale, in this art collection, Little Red and the Wolf, basically, are displayed while they are consuming their own life in a mutual love addiction which is potentially lethal.

They are portrayed as accomplices in the absurdity of their relationship, immersed and alone in their own image. Narcissistically looking at each other, showing themselves as they really are.

Unconsciously, they are overwhelmed by the magmatic background of the wood which swallows them; they're like living stuffed beings in a self-destructive love, willing to be photographed, showing themselves in a decent pose to conceal the unavoidable drama.

Parola Serino captures with an original and perfect style the most significant moment, when the little girl and the wolf enter the labyrinth of the wood, in an evil love which looks like Heaven.

When one goes, one comes.
For each failure there is a success.
When a love ends, another one is coming.
When a friend disappears, another one is looking for you.
For every freezing day, there is a sunny season.
And, remember, do never put the word "ugliness" beside you.

You know what? Your life, the people and the world would be generous
with you
If only you gave them the possibility to show it.
Do something, open the window, create a bit of space, write a poem...
Nothing, like hope, is similar to the love energy.

Enrico Maria Secci

Acknowledgements

The psychologistsValeria Ceci, and Valentina Nichil – Valeria is psychotherapist, trained at the Specialization School in Integrated Strategic Psychotherapy (SCUPSIS), Rome while Valentina is attending the fourth year at the same School – had a crucial role in working on the final draft of this book. Without their patient work of reading and their enthusiasm and professionalism, "Perverse narcissists and the impossible relationships" would have remained just a draft for a long time.

Thanks to Elena Roberta Secci for the editing and her precious advices. Thanks to Paola Serino for the cover photo, taken from her photographic project on love addictions entitled "Wolves", for which I wrote the introduction reported in this book in the final paragraph.

Thanks to those who follow me on Blog Therapy and its Facebook page, to those who attend my seminars, to my courses students and, above all, to all the people I've worked with during therapies: their change and "escape" from impossible relationships allowed me to keep studying and writing with passion and motivation.

Valeria Ceci. Psychologist and psychotherapist specialized in clinical Criminology and in Integrated Strategic Psychotherapy.
She has worked at the University of Bari, with the Professor of Developmental Psychology within the research on prevention of postpartum depression and parenting support.
Consultant Psychologist in several Penitentiary Institutes, Public and Private Schools, trainer of Guidance and Communication in several Training Bodies accredited by the Apulia Region.
She currently works within the planning sector in the schools of Lazio.

Valentina Nichil. Psychologist, she lives and works in Rome. She has a degree in Psychology and is currently attending the fourth year in Integrated Strategic Psychotherapy at the Specialization School in Integrated Strategic Psychotherapy Rome.
She studied parenting support at La Sapienza University, Rome, attending the Postgraduate training course in "Family Enrichment Methods", followed by a second-level Master in Family Mediation at the Institute for Research and Training in Family Mediation (Rome). She currently works as a clinician in public and private institutions also in the other provinces of Lazio.

Elena Roberta Secci. She got a degree in Political Science (history-politics-international study plan) at the University of Cagliari. After a two-year Master's Degree in Journalism in Bologna, she started a personal and professional training course in Rome, from 1998 to 2003, which led her to travel to India, Iraq, Vietnam, Libya, Pakistan, Costa Rica, Egypt and California, France and Belgium, where she had the possibility to learn foreign languages such as English, French and Spanish.

In 1999 she started practicing meditation; she has been practicing a non-postural Yoga from the Kashmir's Shivaite traditions for 16 years, attending several seminars and retreats abroad, especially in USA, Austria, Germany, Switzerland, Spain, Chile and Canada.

In 2003 she studied and started to practice naturopathy. In 2006 she got the degree with full marks after a three-year course at Riza Institute, Milan.

In 2011 she got the first-level Master, magna cum laude in Naturopathy, "La Sapienza" University, Rome.

In 2013 she completed the two-year Master in Yogawellness (yoga therapy and wellness) held by the Italian Yoga Federation in collaboration with the University of Parma.

In 2008 she started holding seminars and conferences on wellness and naturopathic approach to life; she also holds meditation courses in Cagliari, where she currently lives.

Paola Serino. She lives and works in Rome. She has studied photography from 2002 to 2004 at the "Centro Sperimentale di Fotografia Ansel Adams", Rome, and attended workshops held by Leonard Freed, Michael Ackerman and Anders Petersen. After her first works, which were sort of reportages, she has been focusing on portrait photography which she started using as a form of narrative expression.

In 2010 she completed a project at the Dance National Academy in Rome, awarded, in the same year, with the TPW nomination at the contest FNAC "Attenzione Talento Fotografico". Her following works have been awarded and received special mentions in different contests such as the third place at portraits contest of Prix de la Photographie Paris 2013. In 2014 is among the winners of the American Photography Competition. From 2005 she has been showing her works in individual and collective exhibitions.

(website: www.paolaserino.com)

Bibliography

American Psychiatric Association (2014), *DSM-5 – Manuale diagnostic e statistic dei distrubi mentali*, Raffaello Cortina, Milano.

Behary Wendy (2013), *Disarmare il narcisista perverso*, ISC Editore, Firenze.

Bettelheim B. (1976), *Il mondo incantato*, Feltrinelli, Milano.

Berne E. (1972), *Ciao … e poi?*, Bompiani, Milano.

Carter L. (2010), *Difendersi dai narcisisti*, Tea Editore, Milano.

Deetjens M.C. (2009), *Dire basta alla dipendenza affettiva*, Il Punto d'Incontro, Vicenza.

Freud S. (1914), *Introduzione al Narcisismo*, Bollati Boringheri, Torino.

Fisher J. (2001), *L'ospite inatteso. Dal narcisismo al rapporto di coppia*, Raffaello Cortina, Milano.

Gabbard G.O (1995), *Psichiatria psicodinamica*, Raffaello Cortina Editore, Milano.

Gruberger B. (1998), *Il narcisismo*, Einaudi, Milano.

Guerreschi G. (2005), *New Addictions. Le nuove dipendenze*, Edizioni San Paolo, Milano.

Inama L. (2002), *Liberarsi dal troppo amore*, Centro Studi Erickson, Milano.

Rigliano P., Graglia M. (a cura di) (2006), *Gay e lesbiche in psicoterapia*, Raffaello Cortina, Milano.

Manzano J., Palacio E. (2006), *La dimensione narcisistica della personalità*, Franco Angeli Milano.

Lowen A. (1983), *Il narcisismo. La personalità rinnegata*, Feltrinelli, Milano.

Kernberg O.F. (1975), *Sindromi marginali e narcisismo patologico*, Bollati Boringhieri, Torino.

Kernberg O.F. (1984), *Disturbi gravi della personalità*, Bollati Boringhieri, Torino.

Klosko J.S, Young J. (2004), *Reinventa la tua vita*, Raffaello Cortina, Milano.

Kohut H. (1971), *Narcisismo e analisi del Sé*, Bollati Boringhieri, Torino.

Kohut H. (1977), *La guarigione del Sé*, Bollati Boringhieri, Torino.

Nardone G., Watzlawick P. (1990), *L'arte del cambiamento, manuale di terapia strategica e ipnoterapia senza trance*, Ponte alle Grazie, Firenze.

Norwood R. (1989), *Donne che amano troppo*, Feltrinelli, Milano.

O'Halnon B., Fantechi C. (2005), *Dire, fare cambiare. Guida pratica in terapia e nella vita quotidiana*, Franco Angeli, Milano.

O'Halnon B., Beadle S. C. (2005), *Pscoterapia Breve. 51 metodi semplici ed efficaci*, Franco Angeli, Milano

Telfener U. (2014), *Ho sposato un narciso. Manuale di sopravvivenza per donne innamorate*, Castelvecchi Editore, Roma.

Pietro D. (2005), *La dipendenza affettiva. Come riconoscerla e liberarsene*, Edizioni Paoline, Roma.

Secci E.M. (2005), *Manuale di psicoterapia Strategica*, Firera e Liuzzo Edizioni, Napoli.

Secci E.M. (2009), *Blog Therapy. Psicologia e psicopatologia dell'Amore ai tempi di Internet*, Boopen, Napoli.

Secci E.M. (2011), *Aforisimi e metafore per cambiare*, Autorinediti, Napoli.

Secci E.M. (2016), *Le tattiche del cambiamento. Manuale di psicoterapia Strategica*, Youcanprint, Lecce.

Secci E.M. (2016), *"Gli uomini amano poco" – Amore, coppia, dipendenza*, Youcanprint, Lecce.

Secci E.M. (2013), *Aforismi Terapeutici*, Autorinediti, Napoli.

Watzlawick, P., Weakland J.H. (1978), *La prospettiva relazionale*, Astrolabio, Roma.

Watzlawick, P. (1980), Il linguaggio del cambiamento: elementi di comunicazione terapeutica, Feltrinelli, Milano.

White M. (1992), *La terapia come narrazione*, Astrolabio, Roma.

About the author

Enrico Maria Secci was born in Cagliari in 1975. After the Degree Magna cum Laude in Psychology, 1998, he continued his study path at the Institute for Research on Psychotherapies, Rome, a four-year Specialized school in Brief Psychotherapy and Strategic Approach, where he got the Degree of Specialization with full marks and the license to practice Psychotherapy.

He continued his study path at the "Università Cattolica del Sacro Cuore", Rome, in Psychology and Psychotherapy of Addictive Behaviors and related pathologies, Addictions to Alcohol and Drugs and "No-drug addiction": love, sexual, Internet (chats, online auctions) and gambling addictions.

Besides his private practice as a clinician, where he deals with anxiety, depression and other disorders, he has been carrying out an intense teaching and research activity. He collaborates as Didactic Psychotherapist with the Institute for Psychotherapies and is Supervisor and Teacher of Strategic Psychotherapy Techniques at the Integrated Strategic Psychotherapy School in Rome.

In 2012 he started to collaborate as scientific director for Ebookecm Editore's Psychology Series (www.ebookecm.it).

Books, articles, publications

Among the numerous publications within the clinical and psychotherapy field – articles, researches, essays and speeches at conferences and seminars -, he has published:

Aforismi Terapeutici, Edizioni Autorinediti, Napoli, 2013.

Gli uomini amano poco - Amore, coppia dipendenza, Youcanprint, Lecce, 2016.

Le Tattiche del Cambiamento - Manuale di Psicoterapia Strategica, Prometeo, Cagliari, 2011, ebook format accredited by the Ministry www.ebookecm.it

Aforismi e Metafore per Cambiare, Edizioni Autorinediti, Naples, 2011.

Blog-Therapy. Psicologia e psicopatologia dell'Amore ai tempi di Internet, Edizioni Boopen, Naples, 2009.

(con Carlo Duò), *La Comunicazione Strategica nelle professioni sanitarie*", Edizioni Prometeo, Cagliari.(2008), new edition in ebook format accredited by the Ministry, www.ebookecm.it

Manuale di Psicoterapia Strategica, Edizioni Carlo Amore, Rome, 2005.

Contacts

E-mail: enricomariasecci@tiscali.it

Website/blog: www.enricomariasecci.blog.tiscali.it

Facebook: Blog Therapy

Enrico Maria Secci Psicologo Psicoterapeuta Autore

youcanprint

Finito di stampare nel mese di Luglio 2016
per conto di Youcanprint *Self-Publishing*

www.ingramcontent.com/pod-product-compliance
Lightning Source LLC
Chambersburg PA
CBHW062057270326
41931CB00013B/3109